House of Commons Library Documents

PUBLISHED BY HER MAJESTY'S STATIONERY OFFICE

GENERAL EDITOR: DAVID MENHENNET

Number	Title	Date of Publication
1	Acts of Parliament: some Distinctions in their Nature and Numbering	1955
2	A Bibliography of Parliamentary Debates of Great Britain	1967 (reprinted)
3	The Mace in the House of Commons	1971(revised)
4	Official Dress worn in the House of Commons	1960
5	Access to Subordinate Legislation	1963
6	Ceremonial in the House of Commons	1967(reprinted)
7	The Journal of the House of Commons: a Bibliographical and Historical Guide	1971
8	Votes and Standing Orders of the House of Commons: The Beginning	1971
9	Erskine May's Private Journal 1857–1882: Diary of a Great Parliamentarian	1972
10	William Lambarde's Notes; on the Procedures and Privileges of the House of Commons	1977
11	Ceremonial and the Mace in the House of Commons	1980
12	Erskine May's Private Journal 1883–1886	1984
13	Serjeant for the Commons	1986
14	Secretaries to Mr Speaker	1986
15	English Constituency Histories 1265–1832	1986

House of Commons Library Document No 15

English Constituency Histories 1265–1832

A guide to printed sources
by
Janet Seaton
House of Commons Library

R 328.023

London
Her Majesty's Stationery Office
1986

£9.10

CONTENTS

CONTENTS

vi

CONTENTS

CONTENTS

FOREWORD

The author of *English Constituency Histories 1265–1832* has for some years been working in the Home Affairs Section of the Research Division of the House of Commons Library, where among her many responsibilities has been answering questions by Members about the history of their constituencies. This compilation therefore is based on hard experience. But it is more than that because Miss Seaton recently submitted her work in this area for a Fellowship of the Library Association and the reader will not be surprised to learn that she was successful.

It seemed sensible therefore that such an important aid to the study of Parliament and indeed politics should be made more widely available and the House of Commons Library Document Series is a publishing project designed to meet just such an objective. The House of Commons Library is very pleased to add this bibliography to their series and has no doubt that a Library tool that is in such regular use by staff of the House of Commons will be of help to others.

Dermot Englefield
Deputy Librarian

September 1986

INTRODUCTION

Members of Parliament are often interested in their predecessors, and it was in the course of my research on their behalf that I became aware that there was no source that brought together information on constituency histories. Indeed, for the period prior to 1832, there was not even a list of those constituencies that had sent representatives to Parliament, however briefly. This bibliography attempts to fill these gaps.

It begins in 1265 because Simon de Montfort's Parliament is usually considered to be the first that was summoned for a general political purpose, rather than to discuss a specific issue at the King's request. Since then the history of Parliament, and the country, has been shaped by the representatives of the shires, boroughs, cities and towns who were returned at each election. The whole of the period between 1265 and 1832 was one of relative stability in the number and boundaries of constituencies, although there were several enfranchisements and disfranchisements. Despite increasing disparities in population and flagrant corruption in the pocket boroughs, however, it was not until the Great Reform Act of 1832 that radical changes began to be made to the electoral system. In particular, the 1832 Act began the practice of changing constituency boundaries, which makes tracing the history of later constituencies so complicated. This bibliography, therefore, covers constituencies that were represented between 1265 and 1832.

The ideal constituency history would cover the whole period of its representation, give the dates and candidates of all elections and by-elections, indicating any notable controversies, and include detailed biographies of all the MPs. By way of background it should discuss the nature of the franchise, the methods of election, the influence of local families, the extent of patronage, and the general character of the place at different periods. Examples of this ideal are rare, especially in respect of the larger constituencies such as counties, most of which have been continuously represented since the thirteenth century. Nevertheless, there are many studies which are contributions towards the history of a particular constituency. They may be simply a list of representatives, perhaps with biographical notes, or a study of a short period or even a single election. The arrangement of the bibliography by constituency makes it easy to see at a glance whether the definitive work has yet to be written.

Up to the end of the nineteenth century much of the work on the history of particular constituencies was done by amateur local historians with leisure and private means at their disposal. In the twentieth century their role has been almost entirely superseded by the work of large-scale co-operative enterprises such as the Victoria County History and the History of Parliament Trust. In both these cases the research is undertaken by professionals or semi-professionals, most of whom are paid for their contributions. In the V.C.H., the history of constituencies is only one aspect of the local histories which are prepared. With the H.O.P.T., on the other hand, the history of each constituency is an integral part of their study of the personnel of the House of Commons. These contributions are invaluable, and have been indexed in this bibliography in detail.

The approaches of the V.C.H and the H.O.P.T. also represent the two focusses of interest brought together in the study of a constituency history—the local and the national. Finding out who represented an area can bring to life the local effects of the great national issues of the day, and provide a unique picture of the local power structure. At the national level, on the other hand, the history of Parliament itself can be greatly illuminated by the study of the personalities who took part in it over the centuries. It is the combination of these two approaches that makes constituency histories so interesting.

Parliamentary papers, which are adequately indexed already both by subject and by place-name, are not included in this work, with two exceptions. The first is the Official Return of Members of Parliament (item 28 in the bibliography); the second, the Interim Report of the Committee on House of Commons Personnel and Politics (item 27). The Official Return, published between 1878 and 1891, reprinted, Parliament by Parliament, the names of all those known to have been elected since 1213. It was an enormous achievement, and although it has been shown to have errors and omissions, it is still the basic source for many constituency histories. Its publication prompted many local historians to extract the names of the MPs for their area and stimulated interest in further research in this field, which led to many constituency histories being produced around the turn of the century.

Forty years after the publication of the Official Return, the Committee on House of Commons Personnel and Politics surveyed the literature on the history of Members of Parliament and found it wanting. The Committee was chaired by Josiah Wedgwood, MP, who had spent many years compiling his own constituency history of Staffordshire (item 694). This experience had convinced him of the need for a complete history of the personnel of Parliament, and he felt that a great parliamentary history would help to increase Parliament's prestige. The Committee recommended that such a history should be undertaken, and this led eventually to the setting up of the History of Parliament Trust in 1940. The Wedgwood Committee's report remains a landmark in the literature of constituency histories.

Finally, a word about scope and arrangement. The bibliography is limited to England. This is regrettable, but it was the only way to make the field more manageable. The entries themselves are confined to printed sources, which are the most readily available to a wide audience. There is of course a wealth of relevant material in theses, and in local and national archives, but for practical purposes they are relatively inaccessible. The bibliography begins with a section on works which cover a number of constituencies. The most useful of these general sources have been given full cross-references to each constituency covered. The remaining entries are arranged in alphabetical order of counties, and within that in alphabetical order of the represented boroughs. In addition, there are two "non-county" sections on the Cinque Ports and the Universities. At the beginning of each entry there are cross-references, shown in bold type. In some cases these are the only entries for that constituency, but this does not indicate a dearth of material, rather that it is scattered in works which may be devoted to other areas. All names of authors and constituencies appear in the index.

This work will be of interest not only to Members of Parliament, but also to all those studying political and electoral history, and to local historians everywhere. As the first attempt at a comprehensive bibliography in this field, it is bound to be incomplete. Information about additional printed sources will be more than welcome, and perhaps the gaps in the literature which are revealed here can then be filled. Details should be sent to the author at the House of Commons Library, London SW1A 0AA.

Janet Seaton
September 1986

ABBREVIATIONS

Arch.	Archaeological
Assn.	Association
B.	Bulletin
B.I.H.R.	Bulletin of the Institute of Historical Research
E.H.R.	English Historical Review
Hist.	Historical
H.O.P.T.	History of Parliament Trust
J.	Journal
Mag.	Magazine
O.R.	Official Return of Members of Parliament
Proc.	Proceedings
Q.	Quarterly
R.	Review
Rept.	Report
Soc.	Society
Trans.	Transactions
U.P.	University Press
V.C.H.	Victoria County History

NOTES

1. The History of Parliament Trust series will eventually cover the period 1386–1832. The following sets, all entitled *The House of Commons*, have so far been published:—

   1509–1558, by S. T. Bindoff. 3 vols. Secker & Warburg, 1982.

   1558–1603, by P. W. Hasler. 3 vols. HMSO, 1981.

   1660–1690, by B. D. Henning. 3 vols. Secker & Warburg, 1983.

   1715–1754, by R. Sedgwick. 2 vols. HMSO, 1970.

   1754–1790, by Sir L. Namier and J. Brooke. 3 vols. HMSO, 1964.

   1790–1820, by R. G. Thorne. 5 vols. Secker & Warburg, 1986.

2. The Victoria County History is published for the University of London Institute of Historical Research by Oxford University Press.

GENERAL WORKS

1. BEAN, WILLIAM WARDELL.
The parliamentary representation of the six northern counties of England
... from 1603 to the general election of 1886. Hull: Charles Henry
Barnwell, 1890.

> Covers the counties of Cumberland, Durham, Lancashire, Northumberland,
> Westmorland and Yorkshire, together with their cities and boroughs. Includes
> biographical notes.

2. BEATSON, ROBERT.
Chronological register of both Houses of the British Parliament, from the
Union in 1708 to the fourth Parliament of the United Kingdom of Great
Britain and Ireland in 1807. 3 vols. London: Longman Hurst Rees &
Orme, 1807.

> Main section of the register contains a list of the Members returned for each
> constituency, in constituency order, with some biographical notes. Vol 1 covers
> 1708–54; vol 2, 1755–1807. Vol 3 refers mainly to Peers but includes a section
> on the dates of earliest returns for each constituency.

3. BOHUN, WILLIAM.
A collection of debates, reports, orders and resolutions of the House of
Commons touching the right of electing Members to serve in Parliament
... London: Bernard Lintott, 1702.

> Covers the period 1690–1700. Too many constituencies are mentioned to list
> separately, but they are all given cross-references.

4. BRADY, ROB.
An historical treatise of English cities and burghs or boroughs ... 2nd ed.
London: D. Browne, 1722.

> Briefly describes the method of returning Members to Parliament in each
> borough. Does not include names.

5. BRITISH REPRESENTATIVE: or, a general list of the knights, commissioners of
shires, citizens and burgesses returned to all the Parliaments of Great
Britain ... London: T. Astley, 1739.

> Refers to Parliaments from 1705–1734. Contains a list of Speakers from 1259
> to 1734. Includes brief notes of each Member's profession or background.

6. CAREW, THOMAS.
An historical account of the rights of elections of the several counties,
cities and boroughs of Great Britain. London: John Nourse, 1755.

> Gives a detailed history of counties and boroughs covering mainly 1600–1754.
> Based on the Commons Journals, so entries focus on electoral disputes and
> similar matters brought before the House. All entries are given cross-
> references.

7. CORBETT, UVEDALE.
An inquiry into the elective franchise of the freeholders of, and the rights
of election for, the corporate counties in England and Wales: also, a
report of the proceedings of the Warwickshire Election Committee, in
1821. London: J. & W.T. Clarke, 1826.

1

Chapters on Bristol, Canterbury, Chester, Coventry, Exeter, Gloucester, Kingston-upon-Hull, Lichfield, Lincoln, London, Newcastle-upon-Tyne, Norwich, Nottingham, Poole, Southampton, Worcester and York; and also on the Warwickshire County election case of 1821.

8. CORBETT, UVEDALE.
Reports of cases of controverted elections in the sixth Parliament of the United Kingdom, by Uvedale Corbett and Edmund Robert Daniell. London: J. & W.T. Clarke, 1821.

Refers to 1819, and includes Barnstaple, Bristol, Camelford, Chester, Evesham, Fowey, Lancaster, Leominster, Milborne Port, Nottingham, Penryn, Reading, Rochester, Shaftesbury, Truro and Worcester.

9. CUNNINGHAM, T.
An historical account of the rights of election of the several counties, cities and boroughs of Great Britain ... 2 vols. London: G. Robinson, J. Robson and J. Sewell, 1783.

Constituencies are shown in alphabetical order, each introduced by a brief description. The date when each was first represented in Parliament is given, together with some details of controverted elections between 1547 and 1783. Limited usefulness.

10. DOUGLAS, SYLVESTER.
The history of the cases of controverted elections which were tried and determined during the first and second sessions of the fourteenth Parliament of Great Britain ... 2nd ed. 4 vols. London: E. & R. Brooke & J. Rider, 1802.

Refers to 1775–76. The cases are too numerous to list separately, but they have all been given cross-references.

11. FOSTER, JOSEPH.
Collectanea genealogica: English and Irish Members from 1529–1881, and a list of the Members of Parliament from 1529–1881, extending from AB to ANG (England) and from AB to BARRY (Ireland). London: Hazell, Watson & Viney, 1882.

Originally published as articles, in monthly parts. Unfinished.

12. FRASER, SIMON.
Reports of the proceedings before Select Committees of the House of Commons in the following cases of controverted elections ... 2 vols. London: J. Murray, 1793.

Refers to 1790–92. Vol 1: Helston, Okehampton, Pontefract, Dorchester, Newark, Orkney and Zetland. Vol 2: Horsham, Sutherland, Honiton, Steyning, Roxburgh, Cirencester.

13. GEORGE, M. DOROTHY.
Elections and electioneering, 1679–81. *E.H.R.*, XLV, 1930 p552–78.

Detailed accounts of elections in Norfolk, Essex, Amersham and Southwark.

14. GLANVILLE, JOHN.
Reports of certain cases, determined and adjudged by the Commons in Parliament, in the twenty-first and twenty-second years of the reign of King James the First. London: S. Baker and G. Leigh, 1775.

> Refers to 1623–4. Includes the boroughs of Amersham, Arundel, Bletchingley, Chippenham, Cirencester, Dover, East Retford, Haverfordwest, Hertford, Malmesbury, Marlow, Monmouth, Newcastle-under-Lyme, Pontefract, Southwark, Stafford, Stockbridge, Wendover and Winchelsea, and the counties of Norfolk, Cambridge, Gloucestershire, Middlesex and Cumberland.

15. GREGO, JOSEPH.
A history of parliamentary elections and electioneering in the old days . . . from the Stuarts to Queen Victoria. London: Chatto and Windus, 1886.

> See in particular:—
> Chapter VI: John Wilkes as a popular representative.
> Chapter VII: Middlesex elections 1768–9.
> Chapter X: The great Westminster election of 1784.

16. HIRST, DEREK.
The representative of the people?: voters and voting in England under the early Stuarts. Cambridge: C.U.P., 1975.

> Includes case studies of disputes over the franchise in Chester, Chippenham, Colchester, Dover, Exeter, Newcastle-under-Lyme, Oxford, Salisbury, Sandwich, Tewkesbury and Warwick.

17. HUGHES, EDWARD.
North country life in the eighteenth century. Vol I, The North-East, 1700–1750. Vol II, Cumberland and Westmorland, 1700–1830. London: O.U.P., 1952.

> Vol I, Chapter VI: Politics
> Vol II, Chapter VIII: Politics 1760–1830.

18. JALLAND, PATRICIA.
Influence of the aristocracy on shire elections in the North of England, 1450–70. *Speculum*, 47, July 1972 p483–507.

> Examines Yorkshire, Northumberland, Cumberland and Westmorland.

19. JUPP, PETER.
British and Irish elections 1784–1831. Newton Abbot: David & Charles, 1973.

> Interesting reprints of contemporary documents relating to various constituencies. All given cross-references.

20. KEELER, MARY FREAR.
The Long Parliament, 1640–1641: a biographical study of its Members. Philadelphia: American Philosophical Society, 1954.

> One section describes each constituency returning Members to the Parliament, all of which have been given cross-references. Another gives biographical details for each Member in alphabetical order.

21. LEWIS, SAMUEL.

A topographical dictionary of England ... 3rd ed. 5 vols. London: S. Lewis & Co., 1835.

> Vol 5 comprises a representative history of England. There is an introductory survey, followed by hand-tinted boundary maps showing the effect of the 1832 Reform Act. These are the best early maps I have found, and have therefore been given appropriate cross-references.

22. LUDERS, ALEXANDER.

Reports of the proceedings in committees of the House of Commons upon controverted elections heard and determined during the present Parliament. 3 vols. London: Edward Brooke, Thomas Whieldon and John Debrett, 1785–90.

> Discusses the cases of: Pontefract, Ipswich, Michell, Downton, Bedford County, Colchester, Ilchester, Lyme, Saltash, Newport, Cricklade, Buckingham County, Seaford, Honiton, Preston, Norwich and Carlisle.

23. NAMIER, LEWIS.

The structure of politics at the accession of George III. 2nd ed. London: Macmillan, 1957 (1968 reprint).

> Includes case-studies of Bristol, Nottingham, Newcastle-upon-Tyne, Canterbury, Coventry, Maldon, Maidstone, St. Albans, Dover; Shropshire and its boroughs:— Shrewsbury, Bridgnorth, Wenlock, Ludlow, Bishop's Castle; the Cornish boroughs of Penryn, Fowey, East and West Looe, Camelford and Grampound; Harwich and Orford. Information relates mainly to the mid eighteenth century.

24. NEALE, JOHN ERNEST.

The Elizabethan House of Commons. Rev. ed. London: Peregrine Books, 1963. (1976 reprint, London: Fontana).

> Ch. 6: The Rutland election of 1601. Also discusses the Cinque Ports (Dover, Hastings, Hythe, New Romney, Rye, Sandwich and Winchelsea); Lancashire; Chichester and Gloucester.

25. O'BYRNE, ROBERT HENRY.

The representative history of Great Britain and Ireland: comprising biographical and genealogical notices of the Members of Parliament from 1547 to 1847. London: John Ollivier, 1848.

> Parts 1 and 2 only published, covering Bedfordshire, Bedford, Berkshire, Abingdon, Reading, Wallingford and Windsor. Each section has lists of MPs, with biographical accounts at the end of each part.

26. OLDFIELD, THOMAS HINTON BURLEY.

The representative history of Great Britain and Ireland. 6 vols. London: Baldwin, Cradock and Joy, 1816.

> Incorporates his earlier work on the history of the boroughs. Chapters on individual English constituencies are in volumes 3, 4 and 5. Information relates to the period c.1600 – c.1800.

27. PARLIAMENT. *House of Commons.*
Interim report of the Committee on House of Commons Personnel and Politics 1264–1832. London: HMSO, 1932 (Cmd 4130).

A feasibility study for the history of Parliament. Includes a list of sources for borough records and references to the main parliamentary histories.

28. PARLIAMENT. *House of Commons.*
Return of the names of every Member returned to serve in each Parliament ... London: HMSO, 1878–1891.
Part 1. Parliaments of England, 1213–1702 (HC69).
Part 2. Parliaments of Great Britain, 1705–1796.
    Parliaments of the United Kingdom, 1801–1874.
    Parliaments and Conventions of the Estates of Scotland, 1357–1707.
    Parliaments of Ireland, 1559–1800 (HC69–I)
Part 3. Index to Part 1, ... with appendix and corrigenda (HC69–II)
Part 4. Index to Part 2, ... with appendix and corrigenda (HC69–III)
    (Published in 1891).

The source for most lists of Members and invaluable starting point for further research.

29. PECKWELL, ROBERT HENRY.
Cases of controverted elections in the second Parliament of the United Kingdom, begun and holden Aug 31, 1802. 2 vols. London: J. Butterworth, 1805–6.

The cases are too numerous to list separately, but all have been given cross-references.

30. PHILBIN, J. HOLLADAY.
Parliamentary representation, 1832 England and Wales. New Haven, Conn: Yale U.P., 1965.

A survey of the state of parliamentary representation from 1816 to 1832. Useful notes on each constituency and the effect of the Reform Act on seats. Dates of first representation not always accurate. Valuable maps show the changes in representation 1831–2.

31. PHILIPPS, JOHN.
Election cases determined during the first session of the fifteenth Parliament of Great Britain, by Committees of the House of Commons ... London: T. Cadell, 1782. (Vol 1 only).

Refers to 1780–81. Covers Sudbury, Milborne Port and Lyme Regis.

32. PHILLIPS, JOHN A.
Electoral behaviour in unreformed England: plumpers, splitters and straights. Princeton, New Jersey: Princeton U.P., 1982.

Discusses Norwich, Maidstone, Northampton and Lewes between 1761 and 1802.

33. RANKIN, MICHAEL HENRY.

Present state of representation in England and Wales ... London; Baldwin and Cradock, 1832.

Describes each constituency, particularly its boundaries and the nature of the franchise. Does not include names of those elected.

34. ROSKELL, JOHN SMITH.

The Commons in the Parliament of 1422: English society and parliamentary representation under the Lancastrians. Manchester: M.U.P., 1954.

Ch.1: The shire elections, includes a discussion of four contested elections:— Nottinghamshire (1427) and Buckinghamshire, Cumberland and Huntingdonshire (1429). Also has biographical notes of the Knights of the Shire and prominent Burgesses in the 1422 Parliament.

35. SMITH, HENRY STOOKS.

The Parliaments of England from 1715 to 1847. 2nd ed. edited by F.W.S. Craig. Chichester: Political Reference Publications, 1973.

Election results arranged by county and borough. Facsimile of the original (1844–50) with additional material by Fred Craig. No name index.

36. VEITCH, GEORGE STEAD.

The genesis of parliamentary reform. London: Constable, 1913 (1965 reprint).

Ch.1 illustrates the need for reform by reference to examples from Cornwall, Lancashire, Yorkshire, Old Sarum, Dunwich, Appleby, Scarborough, Winchester, Derby, Portsmouth, Cambridge, Lymington, Droitwich and Honiton.

37. WALCOTT, ROBERT.

English politics in the early eighteenth century. Oxford: O.U.P., 1956.

Discusses party and political groupings. Appendix II: Representation of government boroughs, contains lists of those elected, with brief biographical notes, for: Queenborough, Portsmouth, Plymouth, Rochester, Newport (IOW), Newtown (IOW), Yarmouth (IOW); Cinque Ports of Dover, Hastings, Hythe, New Romney, Rye, Sandwich, Seaford & Winchelsea; Preston, Windsor, Harwich, Weymouth & Melcombe Regis, Southampton, Shoreham, Arundel, and Westminster.

38. WEDGWOOD, JOSIAH CLEMENT.

The history of Parliament. 2 vols. London: HMSO, 1936–8.

The forerunner of the History of Parliament Trust series. Vol 1: Biographies of Members of the Commons House, 1439–1509. Vol 2: Register of the Ministers and Members of both Houses, 1439–1509. Section II of Vol 2 lists the Members for each constituency, showing in which Parliaments they sat. Valuable, but the biographies should be used with care as inaccuracies have been found.

39. WHITWORTH, CHARLES.
The succession of parliaments; being exact lists of the Members chosen at each General Election from the Restoration to the last General Election, 1761, with other useful matters. London: R. Davis, 1764.

No biographical information. Includes a name index. Each constituency has been given a cross-reference.

40. WILLIS, BROWNE.
Notitia parliamentaria: or an history of the counties, cities and boroughs in England and Wales. 3 vols. London: Robert Gosling, 1715–50. (2nd ed., vol 2, 1730).

A classic of its time. Gives the history of each borough, with an account of the franchise and lists of MPs. Much more detail on counties and their boroughs, A to D. Not always accurate.

BEDFORDSHIRE

See **2–3, 6, 19–22, 25–6, 30, 35, 38–40.**

41. BASSETT, MARGERY.
Knights of the Shire for Bedfordshire during the middle ages. Luton: Bedfordshire Hist. Record Soc., 1949 (Vol XXIX).

Covers the county, 1265–1504, with detailed biographies.

42. FLETCHER, MARGERY.
A study of Knights of the Shire returned to Parliament by Bedfordshire during the middle ages. *B.I.H.R.*, XII, 1934 p54–6.

Thesis summary.

43. GODBER, JOYCE.
History of Bedfordshire, 1066–1888. Bedford: Bedfordshire County Council, 1969.

References to parliamentary history scattered throughout the book.

44. H.O.P.T.
1509–1558 I, p29–30
1558–1603 I, p111–2
1660–1690 I, p125–6
1715–1754 I, p189–90
1754–1790 I, p205–6
1790–1820 II, pl-4

45. V.C.H. BEDFORDSHIRE.
Vol II, 1908. p17–72.

Covers 1213–1895. Includes general comments on boroughs.

BEDFORD

See **2–3, 6, 10, 20–1, 25–6, 30, 35, 38–40, 45.**

46. FARRAR, C.F.
Old Bedford: the town of Sir William Harper, John Bunyan and John Howard the philanthropist. Bedford: F.R. Hockliffe, 1926.

Ch. XLII: The election of 1830 (p256–9)

47. FLICK, CARLOS T.
The Bedford election of 1830. *Bedfordshire Hist. Record Soc.,* 49, 1970 p160–70.

48. H.O.P.T.
1509–1558 I, p30–1
1558–1603 I, p112–3
1660–1690 I, p126–8
1715–1754 I, p190–1
1754–1790 I, p206–8
1790–1820 II, p4–6

49. MUGGERIDGE, R.M.
A history of the late contest for the representation of the borough of Bedford. London: J. Hatchard & Son, 1830.

Contemporary account of the 1830 general election contest.

50. V.C.H. BEDFORDSHIRE
Vol III, 1912 p20–1.

Covers 1295–1832.

BIGGLESWADE

O.R. only (Members returned in 1275).

DUNSTABLE

See **45.**

51. V.C.H. BEDFORDSHIRE
Vol III, 1912 p361–2.

Covers 1311–12.

ODELL

O.R. only (Members returned in 1275).

SHEFFORD

O.R. only (Members returned in 1275).

BERKSHIRE

See **2–3, 6, 20–1, 25–6, 30, 35, 38–40.**

52. H.O.P.T.
    1509–1558 I, p31–2
    1558–1603 I, p113–4
    1660–1690 I, p128–9
    1715–1754 I, p191–2
    1754–1790 I, p208–9
    1790–1820 II, p6–9

53. JONES, J.E.
The parliamentary representation of Berkshire and its boroughs during the reign of Elizabeth I. *Berkshire Arch. J.,* 63, 1967–8 p39–56.

    Good survey. Covers all boroughs except Newbury.

54. READING OBSERVER.
Members of Parliament for the constituencies of Berkshire, from 1213–1880, with notes. Reading: Reading Observer, 1883.

    Covers all boroughs.

55. V.C.H. BERKSHIRE
Vol II, 1907 p115–166.

    Covers 1265–1832. Includes boroughs, but not in detail.

ABINGDON

See **2–3, 6, 10, 19–21, 25–6, 30, 35, 39–40, 53–5.**

56. BAKER, AGNES C.
Historic Abingdon: parliamentary history and notes on MPs 1588–1714. Abingdon: Abbey Press, 1963.

57. GRUENFELDER, JOHN K.
The spring 1640 parliamentary election at Abingdon. *Berkshire Arch. J.,* 65, 1970 p41–7.

58. H.O.P.T.
    1509–1558 I, p32
    1558–1603 I, p114
    1660–1690 I, p129–30
    1715–1754 I, p192
    1754–1790 I, p209–10.
    1790–1820 II, p9–11

59. TOWNSEND, JAMES.
A history of Abingdon. London: Henry Frowde, 1910.

    References scattered throughout the book.

60. V.C.H. BERKSHIRE
Vol IV, 1924 p441–2.

NEWBURY

See **54−5.**

61. V.C.H. BERKSHIRE
Vol IV, 1924 p137, 145.

READING

See **2−3, 6, 8, 20−1, 25−6, 30, 35, 38−40, 53−5.**

62. ASPINALL, A.
Parliament through seven centuries: Reading and its MPs, by A. Aspinall and others. London: Cassell, 1962.

Covers the period 1295−1959.

63. CHILDS, W. M.
The town of Reading during the early part of the nineteenth century. Reading: University College, 1910. (University College Reading Studies in Local History).

Section on politics of the period, p59−67. Covers 1800−1849.

64. GUILDING, J. M.
Notable events in the municipal history of Reading. Reading: Bradley & Son, 1895.

Members 1800−1895 listed in an Appendix.

65. H.O.P.T.
1509−1558 I, p34−5
1558−1603 I, p115−6
1660−1690 I, p132−3
1715−1754 I, p193−4
1754−1790 I, p211−2
1790−1820 II, p13−15

66. V.C.H. BERKSHIRE
Vol III, 1923 p360−3.

WALLINGFORD

See **2−3, 6, 20−1, 25−6, 30, 35, 38−40, 53−5.**

67. HEDGES, JOHN KIRBY.
The history of Wallingford, in the county of Berks. 2 vols. London: William Clowes & Sons, 1881.

Vol II includes a section on parliamentary representation (p199−212), with a list of MPs, 1302−1880.

68. H.O.P.T.
 1509–1558 I, p35–6
 1558–1603 I, p116–7
 1715–1754 I, p194–5
 1754–1790 I, p212–3
 1790–1820 II, p15–16

69. SMITH, E. ANTHONY.
 Bribery and disfranchisement: Wallingford elections 1820–1832. *E.H.R.*,
 75 (297), 1960 p618–30.

70. V.C.H. BERKSHIRE
 Vol III, 1923 p534–5.

WINDSOR

See **2–3, 6, 20–1, 25–6, 29–30, 35, 37–40, 53, 55.**

71. BOND, SHELAGH.
 A list of Windsor representatives in Parliament 1302–1966. *Berkshire
 Arch. J.* 62, 1965–6 p34–44.

72. H.O.P.T.
 1509–1558 I, p32–4
 1558–1603 I, p115
 1660–1690 I, p130–2
 1715–1754 I, p192–3
 1754–1790 I, p210–1
 1790–1820 II, p11–13

73. V.C.H. BERKSHIRE
 Vol III, 1923 p62–5.

BUCKINGHAMSHIRE

See **2–3, 6, 20–2, 26, 30, 34–5, 38–40.**

74. BROAD, JOHN.
 Sir John Verney and Buckinghamshire elections, 1696–1715. *B.I.H.R.*,
 LVI, 1983 p195–204.

75. DAVIS, RICHARD W.
 Political change and continuity 1760–1885: a Buckinghamshire study.
 Newton Abbot: David & Charles, 1972.

  Discusses all the boroughs as well as the county.

76. H.O.P.T.
 1509–1558 I, p36–7
 1558–1603 I, p117–8
 1660–1690 I, p135–7
 1715–1754 I, p195–6
 1754–1790 I, p213–4
 1790–1820 II, p16–19

77. MUNDEN, R.C.
The defeat of Sir John Fortescue: court versus country at the hustings?
E.H.R., 93, October 1978 p811−6.

Refers to the election of 1604.

78. V.C.H. BUCKINGHAM
Vol IV, 1927 p521−52.

Covers 1290−1906, including boroughs.

AMERSHAM

See **2−3, 6, 13−14, 20, 26, 30, 35, 39−40, 75, 78.**

79. H.O.P.T.
1660−1690 I, p137−8
1715−1754 I, p196
1754−1790 I, p214
1790−1820 II, p19

80. V.C.H. BUCKINGHAM
Vol III, 1925 p145−6.

AYLESBURY

See **2−3, 6, 20−1, 26, 29−30, 35, 39−40, 75, 78.**

81. GIBBS, ROBERT.
A history of Aylesbury with its boroughs and hundreds. Aylesbury:
Robert Gibbs, 1885.

Includes chapters on parliamentary representation arranged by reign. No
index.

82. H.O.P.T.
1509−1558 I, p37−8
1558−1603 I, p118−9
1660−1690 I, p138−9
1715−1754 I, p196−7
1754−1790 I, p214−5
1790−1820 II, p19−22

83. V.C.H. BUCKINGHAM
Vol III, 1925 p9, 11.

BUCKINGHAM

See **2−3, 6, 20−1, 26, 30, 35, 39−40, 75, 78.**

84. H.O.P.T.
1509−1558 I, p38−9
1558−1603 I, p119
1660−1690 I, p139−42
1715−1754 I, p197
1754−1790 I, p215−6
1790−1820 II, p22−3

85. WILLIS, BROWNE.
The history and antiquities of the town, hundred, and deanery of Buckingham. London: the author, 1755.

Ch.VII includes a list of names, 1545–1734.

86. V.C.H. BUCKINGHAM
Vol III, 1925 p478–9.

HIGH WYCOMBE

See **2–3, 6, 20–1, 26, 30, 35, 38–40, 75, 78.**

87. ASHFORD, L.J.
The history of the borough of High Wycombe: from its origins to 1880. London: R.K.P, 1960.

Chapters 6 and 7: The Parliamentary Borough.

88. H.O.P.T.
1509–1558 I, p39–40
1558–1603 I, p119–20
1660–1690 I, p142–3
1715–1754 I, p197–8
1754–1790 I, p216
1790–1820 II, p23–4

89. V.C.H. BUCKINGHAM
Vol III, 1925 p121.

MARLOW

See **2–3, 6, 14, 20–1, 26, 30, 35, 39–40, 75, 78.**

90. FREAR, MARY RENO.
The election at Great Marlow in 1640. *J. of Modern History*, XIV (4), 1942, p433–48.

91. H.O.P.T.
1660–1690 I, p143–4
1715–1754 I, p198–9
1754–1790 I, p216–7
1790–1820 II, p24–6

WENDOVER

See **2, 6, 14, 20, 26, 30, 35, 39–40, 75, 78.**

92. H.O.P.T.
1660–1690 I, p144–5
1715–1754 I, p199–200
1754–1790 I, p217
1790–1820 II, p26

93. V.C.H. BUCKINGHAM
Vol III, 1925 p22–3.

CAMBRIDGESHIRE

See **2−3, 6, 14, 19−21, 26, 30, 35, 38−40.**

94. CARTER, EDMUND.
The history of the county of Cambridge, from the earliest account to the present time. London: S. & R. Bentley, 1819.

Includes a list of MPs for the county and for Cambridge town, 1660−1818.

95. COOK, D.
The representative history of the county, town, and university of Cambridge, 1689−1832. *B.I.H.R.,* XV, 1937, p42−4.

Thesis summary.

96. H.O.P.T.
1509−1558 I, p40−1
1558−1603 I, p120−1
1660−1690 I, p145−7
1715−1754 I, p200
1754−1790 I, p217−8
1790−1820 II, p26−30

97. TAYLOR, MARY M.
Parliamentary elections in Cambridgeshire, 1332−38. *B.I.H.R.*, XVIII, 1940 p21−6.

98. V.C.H. CAMBRIDGE
Vol II, 1948 p377−419.

Parliamentary representation in separate sections. County only.

99. VIRGOE, ROGER.
The Cambridgeshire election of 1439. *B.I.H.R.*, XLVI, May 1973 p95−101.

CAMBRIDGE

See **2−3, 6, 20−1, 26, 30, 35−6, 38−40, 94−5.**

100. H.O.P.T.
1509−1558 I, p41−3
1558−1603 I, p121
1660−1690 I, p147−8
1715−1754 I, p200−1
1754−1790 I, p218−9
1790−1820 II, p30−2

101. TREVELYAN, GEORGE MACAULAY.
The general election at Cambridge, 1705. *Cambridge R.*, L, 1929 p458.

102. V.C.H. CAMBRIDGE
Vol III, 1959 p68–76.

CAMBRIDGE UNIVERSITY

See **2–3, 6, 20–1, 26, 30, 35, 39–40, 95, 983–4.**

103. H.O.P.T.
1660–1690 I, p148–50
1715–1754 I, p201–2
1754–1790 I, p219–21
1790–1820 II, p32–6

104. V.C.H. CAMBRIDGE
Vol III, 1959 p86, 191, 212.

Very sketchy.

ELY

105. V.C.H. CAMBRIDGE
Vol IV, 1953 p28.

ISLE OF ELY LIBERTY

O.R. only (Members returned in 1654).

WISBECH

106. GARDINER, FREDERIC JOHN.
History of Wisbech and neighbourhood during the last fifty years, 1848–1898. Wisbech: Gardiner & Co., 1898.

A section on parliamentary elections in the appendix lists MPs, 1660–1895.

107. V.C.H. CAMBRIDGE
Vol IV, 1953 p265–6.

CHESHIRE

See **2, 6, 20–1, 26, 30, 35, 39–40, 441.**

108. H.O.P.T.
1509–1558 I, p43–4
1558–1603 I, p121
1660–1690 I, p151–2
1715–1754 I, p202–3
1754–1790 I, p221
1790–1820 II, p36–7

109. INGHAM, ALFRED.
Cheshire: its traditions and history. Edinburgh: Pillans & Wilson, 1920.

Chs.XII and XIII, which also cover Chester. Also lists MPs for Cheshire constituencies, 1832–1918.

110. ORMEROD, GEORGE.
The history of the County Palatine and city of Chester ... 2nd ed., revised and enlarged by Thomas Helsby. 3 vols. London: George Routledge, 1882.

List of Knights of the Shire, 1546–1874, Vol 1 p80–2. Parliamentary representatives for Chester, 1553–1874, Vol 1 p219–20.

111. PINCKNEY, PAUL J.
The Cheshire election of 1656. *B. of John Rylands Library*, 49, Spring 1967, p387–426.

112. PINK, WILLIAM DUNCOMBE.
Parliamentary representation of Cheshire, by W.D. Pink and A.B. Beavan. *Local Gleanings,* I, p371–81, 405–11.

Covers 1543 to 1660.

113. V.C.H. CHESHIRE.
Vol II, 1979 p98–166.

Covers county and city of Chester, 1543–1974. Includes boundary maps for 1885 and 1965.

CHESTER

See 2–3, 6–8, 16, 20–1, 26, 30, 35, 39–40, 109–10, 113.

114. BASKERVILLE, S.W.
The establishment of the Grosvenor interest in Chester 1710–48. *Chester Arch. Soc. J.,* 63, 1980 p59–84.

115. FENWICK, GEORGE LEE.
A history of the ancient city of Chester from the earliest times. Chester: Phillipson & Golder, 1896.

Ch.VI discusses the city's parliamentary representation and includes a list of Chester MPs from 1833–1895.

116. GRUENFELDER, JOHN K.
The Chester election of 1621. *Trans. of the Historic Soc. of Lancashire and Cheshire*, CXX, 1968 p35–44.

117. HEMINGWAY, JOSEPH.
History of the city of Chester, from its foundation to the present time. 2 vols. Chester: J. Fletcher, 1831.

Chapter on: Political history of the city of Chester, p378–432. Includes list of MPs for the county (1547–1831) and for Chester (1553–1831).

118. H.O.P.T.
1509–1558 I, p44–5
1558–1603 I, p121–2
1660–1690 I, p152–4
1715–1754 I, p203–4
1754–1790 I, p221
1790–1820 II, p37–40

119. O'GORMAN, FRANK.
The general election of 1784 in Chester. *Chester Arch. Soc. J.*, 57, 1970/1971 p41−50.

CORNWALL
See **2, 6, 19−21, 26, 30, 35−6, 38−40, 141, 825.**

120. COATE, MARY.
Cornwall in the great Civil War and Interregnum 1642−1660: a social and political study. Oxford: O.U.P., 1933.

> Includes lists of Cornish MPs in the Short Parliament, Long Parliament and the Convention Parliament (County and all boroughs).

121. COURTNEY, WILLIAM PRIDEAUX.
The parliamentary representation of Cornwall to 1832. London, printed for private circulation, 1889.

> One of the early classic constituency histories. Discusses each of the boroughs in detail as well as the county.

122. ELLIOTT-BINNS, L.E.
Medieval Cornwall. London: Methuen, 1955.

> Brief references to parliamentary representation. Mentions Bodmin, Helston, Launceston, Liskeard, Lostwithiel, Tregony and Truro.

123. GILBERT, C.S.
An historical survey of the county of Cornwall ... 2 vols. Plymouth: J. Congdon, 1817−20.

> Brief section on civil government discusses the representation of Cornwall in general.

124. GLUBB, A. DE C.
When Cornwall had 44 MPs: a tale of times which have vanished. Truro: A.W. Jordan, 1934.

> Mentions all boroughs. Sections on the 1832 election in Liskeard, and the history of Callington.

125. H.O.P.T.
1509−1558 I, p45−6
1558−1603 I, p122−3
1660−1690 I, p154−5
1715−1754 I, p204−5
1754−1790 I, p222
1790−1820 II, p40−1

126. LAWRENCE, WILLIAM THOMAS.
Parliamentary representation of Cornwall: being a record of the electoral divisions and boroughs of the county from 1295 to 1885 ... Truro: Netherton & Worth, 1925.

> Contains sections on each of the boroughs, with lists of Members in chronological order of Parliament. Comprehensive, interesting, and readable. Illustrated. Supersedes Courtney (**122**).

BODMIN

See **2–3, 6, 20–1, 26, 30, 35, 38–40, 120–2, 124, 126.**

127. H.O.P.T.
    1509–1558 I, p46–7
    1558–1603 I, p123
    1660–1690 I, p155–6
    1715–1754 I, p205–6
    1754–1790 I, p222–3
    1790–1820 II, p42–5

128. MACLEAN, JOHN.
Parochial and family history of the parish and borough of Bodmin in the county of Cornwall. London: Nichols & Sons, 1870.

Parliamentary representation mentioned in passing, but list of Burgesses given from 1295–1868, p140–5. Includes separate family histories.

BOSSINEY

See **2, 6, 20, 26, 30, 35, 39–40, 120–1, 124, 126.**

129. H.O.P.T.
    1509–1558 I, p47–8
    1558–1603 I, p123–4
    1660–1690 I, p156–8
    1715–1754 I, p206–7
    1754–1790 I, p223–5
    1790–1820 II, p45–6

CALLINGTON

See **2–3, 6, 20, 26, 30, 35, 39–40, 120–1, 124, 126, 227.**

130. H.O.P.T.
    1558–1603 I, p124–5
    1660–1690 I, p158–9
    1715–1754 I, p207
    1754–1790 I, p225–7
    1790–1820 II, p47–9

CAMELFORD

See **2–3, 6, 8, 20, 23, 26, 30, 35, 39–40, 120–1, 124, 126, 227.**

131. H.O.P.T.
    1509–1558 I, p48–9
    1558–1603 I, p125–6
    1660–1690 I, p159–6
    1715–1754 I, p208
    1754–1790 I, p227
    1790–1820 II, p49–53

DUNHEVED

See **2, 40, 139−42.**

132. H.O.P.T.
    1509−1558 I, p49−50
    1558−1603 I, p126−7

FOWEY

See **2−3, 6, 8, 19−20, 23, 26, 29−30, 35, 39−40, 120−1, 124, 126.**

133. H.O.P.T.
    1558−1603 I, p127
    1660−1690 I, p161−2
    1715−1754 I, p208−9
    1754−1790 I, p227−8
    1790−1820 II, p53−7

134. KEAST, JOHN.
The story of Fowey (Cornwall). Exeter: James Townsend & Sons, 1950.

    References plentiful but scattered.

GRAMPOUND

See **2−3, 6, 20, 23, 26, 35, 39−40, 120−1, 124, 126, 227.**

135. H.O.P.T.
    1509−1558 I, p50−1
    1558−1603 I, p127−8
    1660−1690 I, p162−3
    1715−1754 I, p209−12
    1754−1790 I, p228−9
    1790−1820 II, p57−62.

136. JASPER, R.C.
Edward Eliot and the acquisition of Grampound. *E.H.R.*, LVIII, 1943, p475−81.

HELSTON

See **2−3, 6, 10, 12, 19−21, 26, 30, 35, 38−40, 120−2, 124, 126.**

137. H.O.P.T.
    1509−1558 I, p51−2
    1558−1603 I, p128−9
    1660−1690 I, p163−4
    1715−1754 I, p212
    1754−1790 I, p229−30
    1790−1820 II, p62−5

138. Toy, H. Spencer.
A patronage feud in a pocket borough: Helston, Cornwall. *History*, 15, 1930–31 p109–18.

Refers to the Duke of Leeds and Sir Christopher Hawkins in 1813.

LAUNCESTON

See **2–3, 6, 20–1, 26, 30, 35, 38–9, 120–2, 124, 126, 132.**

139. H.O.P.T.
1558–1603 I, p127–7; 133
1660–1690 I, p164–6
1715–1754 I, p212–3
1754–1790 I, p230–1
1790–1820 II, p65–6

140. Peter, Richard.
The histories of Launceston and Dunheved, in the county of Cornwall, by Richard Peter and his son Otho Bathurst Peter. Plymouth: W. Brendon, 1885.

Members for "Dunheved otherwise Launceston" 1295–1880, p387–99.
Members for "Launceston, Newport" 1529–1832, p60–7.

141. Robbins, Alfred F.
Launceston past and present: a historical and descriptive sketch. Launceston: Walter Weighell, 1888.

MPs for Cornwall, Launceston and Newport indexed by name.

142. Toy, Henry Spencer.
The Cornish pocket borough. Penzance: Wordens of Cornwall, 1968.

Concentrates on Launceston in 1832.

LISKEARD

See **2–3, 6, 20–1, 26, 29–30, 35, 38–40, 120–2, 124, 126, 187.**

143. H.O.P.T.
1509–1558 I, p52–3
1558–1603 I, p129–30
1660–1690 I, p166–7
1715–1754 I, p213
1754–1790 I, p231–2
1790–1820 II, p66–9

144. Veitch, George Stead.
William Huskisson and the controverted elections at Liskeard in 1802 and 1804. *Trans. Royal Hist. Soc.,* 4th Series, XIII, 1930 p205–28.

LOOE (EAST)

See **2–3, 6, 20, 23, 26, 30, 35, 39–40, 120–1, 124, 126.**

145. BOND, THOMAS.
Topographical and historical sketches of the boroughs of East and West Looe, in the county of Cornwall. London: J. Nichols & Son, 1823.

Appendix includes lists of MPs for East Looe, 1340–1820 and for West Looe, 1552–1820.

146. BROWNE, A.L.
Corporation chronicles: being some account of the ancient corporations of East Looe and of West Looe in the county of Cornwall. Plymouth: John Smith, 1904.

Ch.16 gives an account of the parliamentary election in East Looe in 1796.

147. H.O.P.T.
1558–1603 I, p130–1
1660–1690 I, p167–8
1715–1754 I, p213–4
1754–1790 I, p232
1790–1820 II, p69–71

LOOE (WEST)

See **2–3, 6, 20, 23, 26, 30, 35, 39–40, 120–1, 124, 126, 145.**

148. H.O.P.T.
1509–1558 I, p60–1
1558–1603 I, p131–2
1660–1690 I, p168–9
1715–1754 I, p214
1754–1790 I, p232–3
1790–1820 II, p71–2

149. MEREWETHER, H.A.
Report of the case of the borough of West Looe, in the county of Cornwall, tried before a committee of the House of Commons, April 18, 1822. London: Henry Butterworth, 1823.

Refers to an election in 1822.

LOSTWITHIEL

See **2–3, 6, 20, 26, 30, 35, 38–40, 120–2, 124, 126.**

150. H.O.P.T.
1509–1558 I, p53–4
1558–1603 I, p132
1660–1690 I, p169–71
1715–1754 I, p215
1754–1790 I, p233
1790–1820 II, p72–3

MICHELL

See **2–3, 6, 20, 22, 26, 30, 35, 39–40, 120–1, 124, 126.**

151. H.O.P.T.
    1509–1558 I, p55–6
    1558–1603 I, p132–3
    1660–1690 I, p171–2
    1715–1754 I, p215–6
    1754–1790 I, p233–4
    1790–1820 II, p73–4

NEWPORT

See **2–3, 6, 20, 26, 30, 35, 39–40, 120–1, 124, 126, 140–1.**

152. H.O.P.T.
    1509–1558 I, p56–7
    1558–1603 I, p133
    1660–1690 I, p172–3
    1715–1754 I, p216
    1754–1790 I, p235
    1790–1820 II, p74–5

PENRYN

See **2–3, 6, 8, 20–1, 23, 26, 29–30, 35, 39–40, 120–1, 124, 126, 227.**

153. H.O.P.T.
    1509–1558 I, p57–8
    1558–1603 I, p134
    1660–1690 I, p173–5
    1715–1754 I, p216–7
    1754–1790 I, p235–7
    1790–1820 II, p75–7

154. RODDIS, ROLAND J.
Penryn: the history of an ancient Cornish borough. Penryn: D. Bradford Barton, 1964.

    Ch.X: Parliamentary representation of Penryn. Includes a list of MPs, 1554–1885.

ST. GERMANS

See **2–3, 6, 20, 26, 30, 35, 39–40, 120–1, 124, 126.**

155. H.O.P.T.
    1558–1603 I, p134–5
    1660–1690 I, p175
    1715–1754 I, p217
    1754–1790 I, p237
    1790–1820 II, p77–8

ST. IVES

156. H.O.P.T.
    1509−1558 I, p58
    1558−1603 I, p135
    1660−1690 I, p175−7
    1715−1754 I, p217−8
    1754−1790 I, p237−8
    1790−1820 II, p78−9

157. MATTHEWS, JOHN HOBSON.
A history of Saint Ives, Lelant, Towednack and Zennor, in the county of Cornwall. London: Elliot Stock, 1892.

> Chapter XXXII: Parliamentary history of the borough. Lists MPs, 1558−1874, with biographical notes.

ST. MAWES

158. H.O.P.T.
    1558−1603 I, p135−6
    1660−1690 I, p177−8
    1715−1754 I, p218−9
    1754−1790 I, p239
    1790−1820 II, p80−1

SALTASH

159. CARPENTER, SAMUEL.
A statement of the evidence and arguments of counsel before the Committee of the House of Commons, upon the controverted election for Saltash. London: W. Reed, 1808.

> Discusses previous elections at Saltash.

160. CHRISTIE, IAN R.
Private patronage versus government influence: John Buller and the contest for control of parliamentary elections at Saltash, 1780−1790. *E.H.R.,* 72, 1956 p249−55.

161. H.O.P.T.
    1509−1558 I, p58−9
    1558−1603 I, p136−7
    1660−1690 I, p178−9
    1715−1754 I, p219
    1754−1790 I, p239−40
    1790−1820 II, p81−4

TREGONY

See 2–3, 6, 20, 26, 30, 35, 39–40, 120–2, 124, 126.

162. H.O.P.T.
 1558–1603 I, p137–8
 1660–1690 I, p179–80
 1715–1754 I, p220
 1754–1790 I, p240–1
 1790–1820 II, p84–7

TRURO

See 2–3, 6, 8, 20–1, 26, 30, 35, 38–40, 120–2, 124, 126.

163. H.O.P.T.
 1509–1558 I, p59–60
 1558–1603 I, p138
 1660–1690 I, p180–2
 1715–1754 I, p221
 1754–1790 I, p241–2
 1790–1820 II, p87–8

164. SOME account of the proceedings at the election for Truro, August 3–6, 1830, as reported in the West Briton ... London: Baldwin & Cradock, 1830. (With 3 supplements, 1831–33).

> A collection of newspaper extracts, an account of the election case, letters and a map showing the boundary.

CUMBERLAND

See 1–2, 6, 14, 17–21, 26, 30, 34–5, 38–40.

165. BONSALL, BRIAN.
 Sir James Lowther and Cumberland & Westmorland elections 1754–1775. Manchester: M.U.P., 1960.

> Covers elections in Appleby, Carlisle, Cockermouth, Cumberland, and Westmorland.

166. FERGUSON, RICHARD SAUL.
 Cumberland and Westmorland MPs from the Restoration to the Reform Bill of 1867, (1660–1867). London: Bell & Daldy, 1871.

> Thorough historical section. Includes biographical entries and lists of those elected, arranged by Parliament.

167. H.O.P.T.
 1509–1558 I, p61–2
 1558–1603 I, p139
 1660–1690 I, p182–3
 1715–1754 I, p221
 1754–1790 I, p242–5
 1790–1820 II, p88–91

168. HUDLESTON, CHRISTOPHE ROY.
Papers relating to the Cumberland election of 1768. *Cumberland and Westmorland Antiquarian and Arch. Soc. Trans.,* N.S. Vol 49, 1949 p166–79.

169. V.C.H. CUMBERLAND
Vol II, 1905 p221–330.

Mainly deals with the county. Borough references brief. Appendices list Knights of the Shire 1290–1900 and MPs for each borough.

CARLISLE

See **1–3, 6, 17, 19–22, 26, 30, 35, 38–40, 165–6, 169.**

170. BLAKE, JOYCE.
The story of Carlisle, by Joyce and Brian Blake. Carlisle: City of Carlisle Education Committee, 1958.

Brief section in Chapter VI: How the city has been governed.

171. BROWN, JAMES WALTER.
Round Carlisle cross: old stories retold. Second Series. Carlisle: Charles Thurnam & Sons, 1922.

An election candidate in 1818, p140–5.

172. H.O.P.T.
1509–1558 I, p62–3
1558–1603 I, p139–40
1660–1690 I, p183–5
1715–1754 I, p221–2
1754–1790 I, p245–6
1790–1820 II, p91–4

173. JEFFERSON, SAMUEL.
The history and antiquities of Carlisle. Carlisle: Jefferson, 1838.

Includes list of Carlisle MPs. Volume one of an unfinished history of Cumberland.

174. JOLLIE, FRANCIS.
A political history of the city of Carlisle, from the year 1700 to the present time. Carlisle: F. and J. Jollie, 1820.

Includes details of the elections in 1768, 1816 and 1820.

175. SMITH, M.J.
The mushroom elections in Carlisle, 1784–1803. *Cumberland and Westmorland Antiquarian and Arch. Soc. Trans.,* 81, 1981 p113–21.

COCKERMOUTH

See **1–3, 6, 17, 20–1, 26, 30, 35, 39–40, 165–6, 169.**

176. ASKEW, JOHN.

A guide to the interesting places in and around Cockermouth with an account of its remarkable men and local traditions. 2nd ed. Cockermouth: Evening News, 1872.

Includes chronological list of MPs.

177. BECKETT, J.V.

The making of a pocket borough: Cockermouth 1722–1756. *J. of British Studies*, XX, Fall 1980, p140–57.

178. H.O.P.T.

1660–1690 I, p185–6
1715–1754 I, p222–3
1754–1790 I, p247–8
1790–1820 II, p94

EGREMONT

See **169.**

DERBYSHIRE

See **2, 6, 20–1, 26, 30, 35, 38–40.**

179. GLOVER, STEPHEN.

The history of the county of Derby ...; edited by Thomas Noble. 2 vols. Derby: Stephen Glover, 1829.

Appendix 8 lists Members for Derby Borough from 1294–1826, but gives no biographical details.

180. H.O.P.T.

1509–1558 I, p63–4
1558–1603 I, p140–1
1660–1690 I, p187–8
1715–1754 I, p223
1754–1790 I, p248
1790–1820 II, p94–5

181. V.C.H. DERBYSHIRE

Vol II, 1907 p93–159.

Parliamentary representation covers 1295–1885, with boroughs mentioned briefly.

DERBY

See **2–3, 6, 10, 19–21, 26, 30, 35–6, 38–40, 179, 181.**

182. H.O.P.T.

1509–1558 I, p64–5
1558–1603 I, p141–2
1660–1690 I, p188–9
1715–1754 I, p224
1754–1790 I, p248–9
1790–1820 II, p95

183. HUTTON, W.

The history of Derby from the remote ages of antiquity, to the year 1791. London: J. Nichols, 1791.

Lists the Members for Derby Borough from 1294–1790, with some estimates of the numbers of burgesses. No biographical details are given.

184. SIMPSON, ROBERT.

A collection of fragments illustrative of the history and antiquities of Derby. 2 vols. Derby: G. Wilkins, 1826.

Lists MPs for Derby 1294–1820.

DEVON

See **2–3, 6, 20–1, 26, 30, 35, 38–40, 215.**

185. ALEXANDER, J.J.

Devon county Members of Parliament. Part 1. The early Plantagenet period (1213–1327). *Devonshire Assn. Rept. & Trans.*, XLIV, 1912 p366–81. Part 2. The middle Plantagenet period (1327–1399). Ibid, XLV, 1913 p247–69. Part 3. The later Plantagenet period (1399–1485). Ibid, XLVI, 1914 p478–96. Part 4. The Tudor period (1485–1603). Ibid, XLVII, 1915 p357–71. Part 5. The Stuart period (1603–1688). Ibid, XLVIII, 1916 p320–40. Part 6. The early oligarchic period (1688–1760). Ibid, XLIX, 1917 p363–75. Part 7. The later oligarchic period (1760–1832). Ibid, L, 1918 p589–601. Part 8. Supplement. Ibid, LVII, 1926 p311–20.

186. ALEXANDER, J.J.

First report on the parliamentary representation of Devon. *Devonshire Assn. Rept. & Trans.*, LXII, 1930 p157–60.

Report of a committee set up in response to the Committee on Personnel and Politics (**27**) to search for original records of names and elections.

187. ALEXANDER, J.J.

Second report on the parliamentary representation of Devon. *Devonshire Assn. Rept. & Trans.*, LXV, 1933 p141–6.

Reviews progress from the First report (**186**). Mentions Exeter, Dartmouth, Plymouth, Torrington, Barnstaple, Plympton, Tavistock, Totnes, Dorset, Somerset, Liskeard.

188. ALEXANDER, J.J.

Third report on the parliamentary representation of Devon. *Devonshire Assn. Rept. & Trans.*, LXVI, 1934 p93–104.

Reviews progress since the Second report (**187**). Gives additional information on some Members for the county and for Exeter.

189. ALEXANDER, J.J.

Fourth report on the parliamentary representation of Devon. *Devonshire Assn. Rept. & Trans.*, LXVII, 1935 p145–8.

Reviews what has been published in the way of names and biographies for the county and Barnstaple, Dartmouth, Exeter, Plymouth, Plympton, Tavistock, Totnes, Beeralston, Tiverton, Ashburton, Honiton, Okehampton and Torrington.

190. ALEXANDER, J.J.
Fifth report on the parliamentary representation of Devon. *See* **214.**

191. ALEXANDER, J.J.
Sixth report on the parliamentary representation of Devon. *Devonshire Assn. Rept. & Trans.*, LXIX, 1937 p155–83.

Includes names and information for Devon county, Exeter, Barnstaple, Dartmouth, Plymouth, Plympton, Tavistock and Totnes, some of which is taken from Wedgwood **(38)**.

192. ALEXANDER, J.J.
Seventh report on the parliamentary representation of Devon. *Devonshire Assn. Rept. & Trans.*, LXXI, 1939 p145–66.

Includes a list of Members for Tavistock, 1295–1399 and Torrington, 1295–1369, with biographical notes.

193. ALEXANDER, J.J.
Eighth report on the parliamentary representation of Devon. *Devonshire Assn. Rept. & Trans.*, LXXII, 1940 p117–25.

Covers early returns (1272–1327) relating to the county, Exeter, Honiton, Barnstaple, Plymouth, Torrington, Totnes, and Plympton.

194. ANDRIETTE, EUGENE A.
Members of Parliament for Devon and Exeter, 1640–6. *Devon and Cornwall Notes and Queries,* XXXI, 1968 p47–52.

195. DRAKE, DAPHNE.
Ninth report on the parliamentary representation of Devon. *Devonshire Assn. Rept. & Trans.*, LXXVI, 1944 p75–81.

Surveys what has been published about each of the Devon boroughs (except Blandford). Includes list of Members for Plympton Erle from 1296 to 1485.

196. H.O.P.T.
1509–1558 I, p65–6
1558–1603 I, p142–3
1660–1690 I, p189–91
1715–1754 I, p224
1754–1790 I, p249
1790–1820 II, p95–9

197. HOSKINS, WILLIAM G.
Devon. London: Collins, 1954. (A New Survey of England).

Ch.X: Political and military history. Mentions all boroughs except Blandford and Teignmouth.

198. PEARSON, J.B.
Devonshire in Parliament, 1660–1832. *Devonshire Assn. Rept. & Trans.*, XXX, 1898, p371–7.

Mentions Ashburton, Barnstaple, Beeralston, Dartmouth, Exeter, Honiton, Ilchester, Okehampton, Plymouth, Plympton Erle, Tavistock, Tiverton and Totnes.

ASHBURTON

See **2–3, 6, 20–1, 26, 30, 35, 39–40, 189, 195, 197–8.**

199. HANHAM H.J.
Ashburton as a parliamentary borough, 1640–1868. *Devonshire Assn. Rept. & Trans.*, 98, 1966 p206–56.

200. H.O.P.T.
1660–1690 I, p191–2
1715–1754 I, p224–5
1754–1790 I, p249–50
1790–1820 II, p99–101

201. PEARSON, J.B.
The representatives of the borough of Ashburton. *Devonshire Assn. Rept. & Trans.*, XXVIII, 1896 p219–27.

202. WORTHY, CHARLES.
Ashburton and its neighbourhood: or the antiquities and history of the borough of Ashburton. Ashburton: L.B. Varder, 1875.

Mentioned in briefly in Ch.1.

BARNSTAPLE

See **2–3, 6, 8, 20–1, 26, 29–30, 35, 38–40, 187, 189, 191, 193, 195, 197–8.**

203. DRAKE, DAPHNE.
Members of Parliament for Barnstaple, 1295–1492. *Devonshire Assn. Rept. & Trans.*, LXXI, 1939 p249–65. 1492–1688. Ibid, LXXII, 1940 p251–64. 1689–1832. Ibid, LXXIII, 1942 p181–93.

204. EBRINGTON, *Lord.*
A by-election in 1747. *Nineteenth Century R.*, XXV, p921, 925.

205. GRIBBLE, JOSEPH BESLY.
Memorials of Barnstaple: being an attempt to supply the want of a history of that ancient borough. Barnstaple: J. Avery, 1830.

Ch.III contains a section on the representative history of the borough (p212–44), which includes a list of Members from 1295 to 1826.

206. H.O.P.T.
1509–1558 I, p66–7
1558–1603 I, p143–4
1660–1690 I, p192–4
1715–1754 I, p225
1754–1790 I, p250–1
1790–1820 II, p101–5

BEERALSTON

See **2–3, 6, 20, 26, 30, 35, 39–40, 189, 195, 197–8, 227.**

207. ALEXANDER, J.J.
Bere Alston as a parliamentary borough. *Devonshire Assn. Rept. &
Trans.*, XLI, 1909 p152–78.

208. H.O.P.T.
1558–1603 I, p144–5
1660–1690 I, p194–5
1715–1754 I, p225–6
1754–1790 I, p251
1790–1820 II, p105

BLANDFORD

O.R. only (Members returned in 1275).

BRADNINCH

See **195, 197.**

209. CROSLEGH, CHARLES.
Bradninch: being a short historical sketch of the honor, the manor, the
borough and liberties and the parish. London: De la More Press, 1911.

Brief entry p122–3 describes the election return of 18th March 1314, said to be
the only one.

CREDITON

o   *See* **195, 197.**

DARTMOUTH

See **2–3, 6, 20–1, 26, 30, 35, 38–40, 189, 191, 195, 197–8.**

210. ALEXANDER, J.J.
Dartmouth as a parliamentary borough. *Devonshire Assn. Rept. &
Trans.*, XLIII, 1911 p350–70. Supplementary paper. Ibid, LXI, 1929
p217–8.

211. H.O.P.T.
1509–1558 I, p67–9
1558–1603 I, p145
1660–1690 I, p195–7
1715–1754 I, p226
1754–1790 I, p252–3
1790–1820 II, p106–7

212. RUSSELL, PERCY.
Dartmouth: a history of the port and town. London: Batsford, 1950.

Brief references to parliamentary representation.

213. WATKIN, HUGH R.
Dartmouth. Vol 1: Pre-reformation. Devonshire Association for the
Advancement of Science, Literature and Art, 1935. (Parochial Histories
of Devonshire, No.5).

Lists MPs, 1298–1553, p271–3.

EXETER

See **2−3, 6−7, 16, 20−1, 26, 30, 35, 38−40, 187−9, 191, 193−5, 197−8.**

214. ALEXANDER, J.J.
Exeter Members of Parliament. Part 1. 1295 to 1377. *Devonshire Assn. Rept. & Trans.*, LIX, 1927 p289−309. Part 2. 1377 to 1537. Ibid, LX, 1928 p183−214. Part 3. 1537 to 1688. Ibid, LXI, 1929 p193−215. Part 4. 1688 to 1832. Ibid, LXII, 1930 p195−223. Additions and corrections, Fifth report on the parliamentary representation of Devon. Ibid, LXVIII, 1936 p105−11.

215. CULLUM, R.
The spirit of election wit at the City of Exeter and County of Devon. Exeter: R. Cullum, 1812.

216. H.O.P.T.
1509−1558 I, p69−71
1558−1603 I, p145−7
1660−1690 I, p197−201
1715−1754 I, p226−7
1754−1790 I, p253
1790−1820 II, p107−9

217. MacCAFFREY, WALLACE T.
Exeter, 1540−1640: the growth of an English county town. Cambridge: Harvard U.P., 1958.

Ch.9: The civic community and the Royal government. Sketchy coverage of parliamentary representation.

218. OLIVER, GEORGE.
The history of the city of Exeter. Exeter: William Roberts, 1861.

Ch.V: Representatives of Exeter in Parliament. Includes a list, 1466−1857.

219. SYKES, N.
The Cathedral Chapter of Exeter and the general election of 1705. *E.H.R.*, 45, April 1930 p260−72.

FREMINGTON

See **195, 197.**

HONITON

See **2, 6, 12, 20−2, 26, 29−30, 35−6, 39−40, 189, 193, 195, 197−8, 227.**

220. FARQUHARSON, A.
The history of Honiton. Exeter: the author, 1868.

Ch.III: The borough, includes a list of Members of Parliament and unsuccessful candidates, from 1301 to 1866, with additional notes. Also contains biographies of some Members.

DEVON

221. H.O.P.T.
    1660–1690 I, p201–4
    1715–1754 I, p227
    1754–1790 I, p253–4
    1790–1820 II, p109–13

222. WILKIN, WALTER HAROLD.
    Notes on the Members for Honiton, 1640–1868. *Devonshire Assn. Rept. & Trans.*, LXVI, 1934 p253–78.

LIDFORD

See **195, 197.**

MODBURY

See **195, 197.**

OKEHAMPTON

See **2–3, 6, 12, 20, 26, 29–30, 35, 39–40, 195, 197–8.**

223. BRIDGES, WILLIAM B.
    Some account of the barony and town of Okehampton: its antiquities and institutions. New ed., with additional chapters by W.H.K. Wright. Tiverton: William Masland, 1889.

    Section on parliamentary representation p134–46. Covers 1300–1832; includes a list of names with some notes.

224. H.O.P.T.
    1660–1690 I, p202–4
    1715–1754 I, p227–8
    1754–1790 I, p254–7
    1790–1820 II, p113–7

PLYMOUTH

See **2–3, 6, 20–1, 26, 30, 35, 37, 38–40, 187, 189, 191, 193, 195, 197–8.**

225. GILL, CRISPIN.
    Plymouth: a new history, 1603 to the present day. Newton Abbot: David & Charles, 1979.

    Interesting, quite detailed.

226. H.O.P.T.
    1509–1558 I, p71–2
    1558–1603 I, p147
    1660–1690 I, p204–5
    1715–1754 I, p228–9
    1754–1790 I, p257–8
    1790–1820 II, p118–24

227. WHITFELD, HENRY FRANCIS.

Plymouth and Devonport: in times of war and peace. Plymouth: E. Chapple, 1900.

> Ch.XV. Elections discussed from 1790–1831, in Plymouth and the county. Section on the pocket boroughs around Plymouth 1769–1831 (Camelford, Penryn, Plympton, Honiton, Grampound, Callington, St. Ives, St. Mawes, Beeralston, Saltash). Also covers 1832–1897.

228. WORTH, R.N.

History of Plymouth from the earliest period to the present time. Plymouth: William Brendon & Son, 1890.

> Ch.VIII, Parliamentary representation. Includes a list of MPs, 1298–1886.

PLYMPTON ERLE

See **2–3, 6, 20, 26, 30, 35, 38–40, 187, 189, 191, 193, 195, 197–8, 227.**

229. H.O.P.T.

    1509–1558 I, p72–3
    1558–1603 I, p147–8
    1660–1690 I, p206–7
    1715–1754 I, p229
    1754–1790 I, p258
    1790–1820 II, p124–5

230. ROWE, J. BROOKING.

A history of the borough of Plympton Erle ... in the county of Devon. Exeter: James G. Commin, 1906.

> Ch.IV: Parliamentary representation. Incudes a list of MPs, 1295–1832, interspersed with notes and details of particular elections.

SOUTH MOLTON

See **195, 197.**

TAVISTOCK

See **2–3, 6, 20–1, 26, 30, 35, 38–40, 187, 189, 191–2, 195, 197–8.**

231. ALEXANDER, J.J.

Tavistock as a parliamentary borough. Pt. I, 1295–1688. *Devonshire Assn. Rept. & Trans.*, XLII, 1910 p258–77. Pt II, 1688–1885. Ibid., XLII, 1911 p371–402.

232. H.O.P.T.

    1509–1558 I, p73–5
    1558–1603 I, p148
    1660–1690 I, p207–8
    1715–1754 I, p229–30
    1754–1790 I, p259
    1790–1820 II, p125–6

TEIGNMOUTH

See **195.**

TIVERTON

See **2–3, 6, 20–1, 26, 30, 35, 39–40, 189, 195, 197–8.**

233. CHALK, E.S.
   Notes on the Members for Tiverton (Devon), 1621–1832. *Devonshire Assn. Rept. & Trans.*, LXVII, 1936 p315–47.

234. HARDING, WILLIAM.
   The history of Tiverton, in the county of Devon. 2 vols. Tiverton: F. Boyce, 1845.

   > Difficult to use as page numbers are not continuous, but interesting references can be found from the indexes.

235. H.O.P.T.
   1660–1690 I, p208–9
   1715–1754 I, p230
   1754–1790 I, p259–61
   1790–1820 II, p126–7

236. SNELL, FREDERICK JOHN.
   Memorials of old Devonshire; edited by F.J. Snell. London: Bemrose & Sons, 1904.

   > Tiverton as a pocket borough, p284–96.

237. SNELL, FREDERICK JOHN.
   Palmerston's borough: a budget of electioneering anecdotes, jokes, squibs and speeches. London: Horace Marshall, 1894.

   > Apart from the first chapter (entitled 'Antediluvian politics') the book is mainly devoted to post-1832 events. It is lively and interesting, though lacks an index.

TORRINGTON

See **3, 187, 189, 192–3, 195, 197.**

TOTNES

See **2–3, 6, 20–1, 26, 30, 35, 38–40, 187, 189, 191, 193, 195, 197–8.**

238. H.O.P.T.
   1509–1558 I, p75–6
   1558–1603 I, p148–9
   1660–1690 I, p209–10
   1715–1754 I, p230–1
   1754–1790 I, p261–4
   1790–1820 II, p127–9

239. RUSSELL, PERCY.
The good town of Totnes. Exeter: Devonshire Association for the Advancement of Science, Literature and Art, 1964.

References to parliamentary representation scattered.

240. WINDEATT, EDWARD.
The MPs for the borough of Totnes. *Devonshire Assn. Rept. & Trans.*, XXXII, 1900 p431–53.

List of Members, 1295–1867, with biographical notes.

DORSET
See 2–3, 6, 20–1, 26, 30, 35, 38–40, 187.

241. CLARK, W.
The parliamentary representation of Dorset from the reign of Edward I. *Dorset Year Book*, 1930 p18–21.

242. H.O.P.T.
1509–1558 I, p76–7
1558–1603 I, p149–50
1660–1690 I, p211–2
1715–1754 I, p231
1754–1790 I, p264
1790–1820 II, p129–31

243. HUTCHINS, JOHN.
The history and antiquities of the county of Dorset ... 3rd ed. 4 Vols. London: John Bowyer Nichols & Sons, 1861–73.

Good sections on the parlimentary representation of each of the boroughs, with lists of MPs for each, taken from Willis' Notitia Parliamentaria.

244. V.C.H. DORSET
Vol II, 1908 p123–74.

All boroughs mentioned.

BRIDPORT
See 2–3, 6, 20–1, 26, 30, 35, 38–40, 243–4.

245. H.O.P.T.
1509–1558 I, p77–8
1558–1603 I, p150
1660–1690 I, p212–3
1715–1754 I, p231–2
1754–1790 I, p264–5
1790–1820 II, p131–2

246. W., J.C.
The Bridport precept, 1306. *Somerset and Dorset Notes and Queries*, XXIII, p25–7.

CORFE CASTLE
See 2–3, 6, 20, 26, 30, 35, 39–40, 243–4.

DORSET

247. H.O.P.T.
    1558–1603 I, p150–1
    1660–1690 I, p214–5
    1715–1754 I, p232–3
    1754–1790 I, p265
    1790–1820 II, p132–3

248. MAYO, CHARLES HERBERT.
Election expenses: Corfe Castle, 1784. *Somerset and Dorset Notes and Queries*, VII, p65.

DORCHESTER
See **2–3, 6, 10, 12, 20–1, 26, 30, 35, 38–40, 243–4.**

249. H.O.P.T.
    1509–1558 I, p78–80
    1558–1603 I, p151–2
    1660–1690 I, p215–6
    1715–1754 I, p233–4
    1754–1790 I, p265–6
    1790–1820 II, p133–4

250. MAYO, CHARLES HERBERT.
The municipal records of the borough of Dorchester, Dorset; edited by Charles Herbert Mayo. Exeter: William Pollard & Co., 1908.

Note of records relating to some Dorchester elections, 1620 to 1780.

251. SAVAGE, JAMES.
The history of Dorchester ... Dorchester: G. Clark, 1823.

Section on parliamentary history, p131–43.

LYME REGIS
See **2, 6, 20–2, 26, 30–1, 35, 38–40, 243–4.**

252. H.O.P.T.
    1509–1558 I, p80–1
    1558–1603 I, p152–3
    1660–1690 I, p216–8
    1715–1754 I, p234–5
    1754–1790 I, p266–7
    1790–1820 II, p134

253. ROBERTS, GEORGE.
The history and antiquities of the borough of Lyme Regis and Charmouth. London: Samuel Bagster, 1834.

Includes a list of Members, 1294–1832, p376–81.

MELCOMBE REGIS
See **2–3, 38–40.**

254. H.O.P.T.
    1509–1558 I, p81–2
    1558–1603 I, p155

POOLE

See **2–3, 6–7, 10, 20–1, 26, 30, 35, 38–40, 243–4.**

255. H.O.P.T.
   1509–1558 I, p82–4
   1558–1603 I, p153
   1660–1690 I, p218–9
   1715–1754 I, p235–6
   1754–1790 I, p267–71
   1790–1820 II, p134–9

256. KERR, BARBARA.
Thomas Hyde of Arne and the Poole election of 1768. *Dorset Natural History and Arch. Soc. Proc.*, 89, 1967 p282–96.

257. SYDENHAM, JOHN.
The history of the town and county of Poole. Poole: the author, 1839.

   Section on Parliamentary annals, p244–90, includes a list of representatives, 1340–1834, with some biographical details.

SHAFTESBURY

See **2–3, 6, 8, 10, 20–1, 26, 29–30, 35, 38–40, 243–4.**

258. H.O.P.T.
   1509–1558 I, p84–5
   1660–1690 I, p219–21
   1715–1754 I, p236–7
   1754–1790 I, p271
   1790–1820 II, p139–41

WAREHAM

See **2–3, 6, 20–1, 26, 30, 35, 38–40, 243–4.**

259. H.O.P.T.
   1509–1558 I, p85–6
   1558–1603 I, p154–5
   1660–1690 I, p221–2
   1715–1754 I, p237–8
   1754–1790 I, p272
   1790–1820 II, p141

WEYMOUTH

See **2, 38–40.**

260. H.O.P.T.
   1509–1558 I, p86–8
   1558–1603 I, p155

WEYMOUTH & MELCOMBE REGIS

See **3, 6, 20–1, 26, 29–30, 35, 37, 243–4.**

261. BATTEN, J.
Treating at elections: Weymouth and Melcombe Regis, 1780. *Somerset and Dorset Notes and Queries*, VII p30-1.

262. H.O.P.T.
1558-1603 I, p155-7
1660-1690 I, p222-5
1715-1754 I, p238-9
1754-1790 I, p272-3
1790-1820 II, p141-7

263. MOULE, HENRY JAMES.
Descriptive catalogue of the charters, minute books and other documents of the borough of Weymouth and Melcombe Regis, A.D. 1252 to 1800. Weymouth: Sherren & Son, 1883.

Index contains references to the election and payment of MPs.

264. WEINSTOCK, MAUREEN BESSIE.
More Dorset Studies. Dorchester: Longmans, 1960.

Section on: The defence of the ports and their parliamentary representation, especially p54-6.

DURHAM
See **1-3, 6, 17, 21, 26, 30, 35, 39-40.**

265. FORDYCE, WILLIAM.
The history and antiquities of the County Palatine of Durham. 2 vols. Newcastle upon Tyne: Thomas Fordyce, 1885.

Vol 1 contains sections on the parliamentary representation of both city and county, 1653-1852. Biographical details very brief.

266. H.O.P.T.
1660-1690 I, p225-7
1715-1754 I, p239-40
1754-1790 I, p273-4
1790-1820 II, p148-51

267. KLIENEBERGER, HANS RUDOLF.
Durham elections: a list of material relating to parliamentary elections in Durham, 1675-1874. Durham: University Library, 1959. (Durham University Library Publications No.2).

A bibliography. Section 2: Miscellaneous election literature, covers histories of parliamentary representation in city and county. Also lists poll books, broadsides and manuscript material. Well arranged.

268. MACKENZIE, ENEAS.
An historical, topographical and descriptive view of the County Palatine of Durham, by E. Mackenzie and M. Ross. 2 vols. Newcastle upon Tyne: Mackenzie & Dent, 1834.

Vol I includes an account of the county's parliamentary representation with a list of Members, based on Sir Cuthbert Sharp's work **(269)**. Vol II does the same for the city.

269. SHARP, *Sir* CUTHBERT.
A list of the knights and burgesses who have represented the county and city of Durham in Parliament. 2nd ed. Sunderland: Marwood, 1831.

Names and biographical details of Members for the county from 1653 and for the city from 1654, with an introduction. Includes some portraits and coats of arms.

270. V.C.H. DURHAM
Vol II, 1907 p133−73.

Mainly pre 1660. Parliamentary representation mentioned in passing.

DURHAM CITY

See **1−3, 6, 17, 19, 21, 26, 29−30, 35, 39−40, 265, 267−70.**

271. H.O.P.T.
1660−1690 I, p227−8
1715−1754 I, p240−1
1754−1790 I, p274
1790−1820 II, p151−5

272. HUTCHINSON, WILLIAM.
The history and antiquities of the County Palatine of Durham. 3 vols. Vol I, Newcastle: S. Hodgson, 1785. Vol II, Newcastle: S. Hodgson, 1787. Vol III, Carlisle: F. Jollie, 1794.

Vol 2, p46−7 gives a list of MPs for the City of Durham from 1654−1784. Also mentions an election in 1761. Nothing for the county found.

273. V.C.H. DURHAM
Vol III, 1928 p41.

ESSEX

See **2−3, 6, 13, 19−21, 26, 30, 35, 38−9.**

274. BARRETT-LENNARD, THOMAS.
Some letters concerning Essex elections in the early part of the 18th century. *Essex R.,* 20, 1911 p169−84.

Letters to an Essex squire, mainly about county elections, 1702−1710.

275. BENHAM, WILLIAM GURNEY.
The Essex petition of 1679−80. *Essex R.,* 43, 1934 p193−203.

276. BOHANNON, MARY ELIZABETH.
Essex election of 1604. *E.H.R.* 48, July 1933 p395−413.

277. BROWN, A.F.J.
English history from Essex sources 1750−1900. Chelmsford: Essex County Council, 1952. (Essex Record Office Publications No.18).

Chapter entitled: Essex and national politics, p183−210. Includes references to the boroughs.

278. CAUNT, GEORGE.
Essex in Parliament. Chelmsford: Essex Record Office, 1969.

> Includes information on Colchester and Maldon as well as the county. Covers 1265–1966.

279. COLLER, D.W.
The people's history of Essex. Chelmsford: Meggy & Chalk, 1861.

> Ch.X: The parliamentary franchise in the county and boroughs etc. Brief.

280. EDWARDS, A.C.
A history of Essex with maps and pictures. London: Darwen Finlayson, 1958.

> Ch.XI: Parliamentary representation. Includes map of 1955 boundaries, with earlier notes.

281. FITCH, EDWARD ARTHUR.
Essex elections. *Essex R.,* 2, 1893 p224–30.

> Lists of members elected 1660–1832, for the county and its boroughs.

282. FOWLER, ROBERT COPP.
Essex Members of Parliament. *Essex Arch. Soc. Trans.* N.S. 17, 1926 p37.

> Lists a few names additional to the O.R. for Colchester, Maldon and the county, 1574–89.

283. H.O.P.T.
1509–1558 I, p88–9
1558–1603 I, p157–9
1660–1690 I, p228–30
1715–1754 I, p241
1754–1790 I, p274–6
1790–1820 II, p155–8

284. GRUENFELDER, JOHN K.
The election for the Knights of the Shire for Essex in the spring, 1640. *Essex Arch. Soc. Trans.,* 3rd Ser. II(2), 1968 p143–6.

285. SMITH, HAROLD.
Essex parliamentary elections, Commonwealth and Restoration. *Essex R.,* 33, 1924 p11–14.

> Covers the county only.

286. SMITH HAROLD.
Some Essex parliamentarians 1642–53. *Essex R.,* 33, 1924 p149–55.

> MPs with Essex connections.

287. THOMPSON, C.
The third Lord Rich and the Essex election of 1604. *Essex J.,* 14(1), 1979 p2–6.

288. V.C.H. ESSEX
Vol II, 1907 p203−57.

Parliamentary representation covers mainly 1600−1832, and includes references to boroughs.

COLCHESTER

See **2−3, 6, 16, 20−2, 26, 29−30, 35, 38−40, 277−8, 281−2, 288.**

289. BENHAM, CHARLES E.
Colchester worthies: a biographical index of Colchester. London: Simpkin, Marshall, Hamilton, Kent & Co., 1892.

Lists MPs from 1660−1888 and includes their biographies.

290. BENHAM, *Sir* WILLIAM GURNEY.
A parliamentary election in Colchester in 1571: an electorate of thirty-five. *Essex R.,* XLIX, 1940 p185−90.

291. BROWN, A.F.J.
Colchester 1815−1914. Chelmsford: Essex County Council, 1980. (Essex Record Office Publications, No.74).

Ch.IV: Politics, includes a section on the parliamentary reform movement, 1815−1832.

292. CROMWELL, THOMAS.
History and description of the ancient town and borough of Colchester in Essex. London: Robert Jennings, 1825.

Part II, Ch.V pt 3 discusses Colchester's parliamentary representation. Includes a list of Members from 1294 to 1820.

293. H.O.P.T.
1509−1558 I, p89−90
1558−1603 I, p159−60
1660−1690 I, p230−2
1715−1754 I, p241−2
1754−1790 I, p276−8
1790−1820 II, p158−60

294. MARTIN, GEOFFREY.
The story of Colchester from Roman times to the present day. Colchester: Benham Newspapers, 1959.

Includes references to parliamentary elections.

295. RICKWORD, GEORGE.
Colchester election, 1654. *Essex R.,* 8, 1899 p255.

296. RICKWORD, GEORGE.
Members of Parliament for Colchester.
1547−1558 *Essex R.,* 4, 1895 p110−22
1558−1603 Ibid, p235−45
1603−1683 Ibid, 5, 1896 p193−213
1685−1741 Ibid, 6, 1897 p171−87
1747−1830 Ibid, 8, 1899 p226−41.

297. ROUND, J.H.
Colchester and the Commonwealth. *E.H.R.,* XV, 1900 p641–64.

Discusses Colchester 1642–1660, focussing mainly on municipal government.

HARWICH

See **2–3, 6, 19–21, 23, 26, 29–30, 35, 37, 39–40, 277–8, 281, 288.**

298. H.O.P.T.
1660–1690 I, p232–4
1715–1754 I, p242
1754–1790 I, p278–80
1790–1820 II, p160–1

299. TAYLOR, SILAS.
The history and antiquities of Harwich and Dovercourt, topographical, dynastical and political, enlarged by Samuel Dale. London: C. Davis, 1730.

List of MPs for Harwich 1640–1727, p127–8, with a 'corrected' list, 1343–1727, p450–1.

300. THOMAS, DAVID A.
Samuel Pepys, MP for Harwich. *Essex R.,* 258, Jan 1957 p35–7.

MALDON

See **2–3, 6, 19–21, 23, 26, 29–30, 35, 38–40, 277–8, 281–2, 288.**

301. DILLIWAY, E.
Maldon elections a hundred years ago. *Essex R.,* 51, 1942 p189–93.

Some information about pre-1832 elections included.

302. H.O.P.T.
1509–1558 I, p90–1
1558–1603 I, p160–1
1660–1690 I, p234–6
1715–1754 I, p243
1754–1790 I, p280–1
1790–1820 II, p161–4

GLOUCESTERSHIRE

See **2–3, 6, 14, 20–1, 26, 30, 35, 38–9.**

303. CANNON, JOHN.
Gloucestershire politics 1750–1800. *Bristol and Gloucestershire Arch. Soc. Trans.,* 79, 1960 p293–7.

Covers the county only.

304. GLOUCESTERSHIRE elections of 1640. *Gloucestershire Notes and Queries,* (i) 1881 p410–4.

305. H.O.P.T.
1509–1558 I, p91–2
1559–1603 I, p162
1660–1690 I, p236–7
1715–1754 I, p243–4
1754–1790 I, p281–3
1790–1820 II, p165–7

306. HUDLESTON, CHRISTOPHE ROY.
Gloucestershire voters in 1710, by C.R. Hudleston and R. Austin. *Bristol and Gloucestershire Arch. Soc. Trans. for 1936,* 58, 1937 p195–205.

307. SAUL, NIGEL.
Knights and esquires: the Gloucestershire gentry in the fourteenth century. Oxford: Clarendon Press, 1981.

Parliamentary representation, p119–28. Sketchy.

308. SMITH, BRIAN S.
A history of Bristol and Gloucestershire, by Brian S. Smith and Elizabeth Ralph. Beaconsfield: Darwen Finlayson, 1972.

Ch.XXV: Parliamentary reform. Includes maps of representation in 1300, 1832 and 1885. Covers all boroughs.

309. W., S.
An election performance in Gloucestershire. *Westminster Mag.,* 1776 p479–80.

Relates to the 1776 election.

310. WILLIAMS, WILLIAM RETLAW.
The parliamentary history of the county of Gloucester ... 1213–1898. Hereford: Jakeman & Carver, 1898.

The standard work. Includes chapters on Bristol, Gloucester, Cheltenham, Cirencester, Stroud and Tewkesbury. Members are discussed in chronological order of election.

BRISTOL

See **2–3, 6–8, 10, 20–1, 23, 26, 30, 35, 38–40, 308, 310.**

311. BARKER, W.R.
The Bristol pageant, A.D. 1820. *Proc. Clifton Antiquarian Club,* (vii) 1912 p35–45.

Describes incidents connected with the election of Henry Bright in 1820.

312. BEAVEN, ALFRED BEAVEN.
Bristol lists: municipal and miscellaneous. Bristol: T.D. Taylor, Sons & Hawkins, 1899.

Reprinted from the Bristol Times & Mirror. Members of Parliament for Bristol 1529–1896, p165–75, 428 with additional notes.

313. DRIVER, J.T.
Parliamentary burgesses for Bristol and Gloucester, 1422–1437. *Bristol and Gloucestershire Arch. Soc. Trans.*, LXXXIV, 1955 p60–127.

Covers the boroughs of Bristol and Gloucester.

314. H.O.P.T.
1509–1558 I, p92–5
1558–1603 I, p162–3
1660–1690 I, p237–40
1715–1754 I, p244–5
1754–1790 I, p283–90
1790–1820 II, p167–72

315. HUNT, WILLIAM.
Bristol. London: Longmans, Green & Co., 1887. (Historic Towns series).

Ch.IX: Politics and riots, p190–206 and p85–7.

316. HUTTON, STANLEY.
Bristol and its famous associations. London: Simpkin, Marshall, Hamilton, Kent & Co., 1907.

Ch.VIII: Political associations, p323–36. Discusses famous men connected with Bristol, including Edmund Burke.

317. LATIMER, JOHN.
Annals of Bristol in the seventeenth century. Bristol: William George's Sons, 1900.

Many references to Bristol MPs and elections, but scattered throughout the text. Best picked out via the index.

318. LATIMER, JOHN.
The annals of Bristol in the eighteenth century. Privately printed, 1893.

Brief accounts of each election in the period, in chronological order.

319. LITTLE, BRYAN.
The city and county of Bristol: a study in Atlantic civilisation. London: Werner Laurie, 1954.

References scattered. Best picked out from the index.

320. NICHOLLS, J.F.
Bristol past and present, by J.F. Nicholls and John Taylor. 3 vols. Bristol: J.W. Arrowsmith, 1881–2.

Vol III: Table showing details of Bristol elections, 1734–1880 p232–4.

321. UNDERDOWN, P.T.
Henry Cruger and Edmund Burke: colleagues and rivals at the Bristol election of 1773. *William and Mary Q.*, 15, January 1958 p14–34.

322. UNDERDOWN, P.T.
Bristol and Burke. Bristol: Historical Association Bristol Branch, 1961.

Covers the period 1774–80.

323. WILLIAMS, JEANIE.
Bristol in the general elections of 1818 and 1820. *Bristol and Gloucestershire Arch. Soc. Trans.*, 87, 1968 p173–201.

CIRENCESTER

See **2–3, 6, 12, 14, 20–1, 26, 29–30, 35, 39–40, 308, 310.**

324. BROWNE, A.L.
The Cirencester election of 1695. *Bristol and Gloucestershire Arch. Soc. Trans. for 1935,* 57, 1936 p269–74.

325. H.O.P.T.
1509–1558 I, p95
1558–1603 I, p163–4
1660–1690 I, p240–1
1715–1754 I, p245–6
1754–1790 I, p290
1790–1820 II, p173–4

326. JENNINGS, R.W.
The Cirencester contest and its aftermath: 1754. *Bristol and Gloucestershire Arch. Soc. Trans.*, 92, 1973 p157–68.

GLOUCESTER

See **2–3, 6–7, 20–1, 24, 26, 30, 35, 38–40, 308, 310, 313.**

327. CANNON, JOHN.
The parliamentary representation of the city of Gloucester (1727–1790). *Bristol and Gloucestershire Arch. Soc. Trans.,* 78, 1959 p137–52.

328. FOSBROOKE, THOMAS DUDLEY.
An original history of the city of Gloucester ... London: John Nichols & Son, 1819.

Lists Members for Gloucester from 1294–1818, with a brief note.

329. GOODMAN, GORDON L.
Pre-reform elections in Gloucester city, 1789–1831. *Bristol and Gloucesterhsire Arch. Soc. Trans for 1965,* 84, 1966 p141–60.

330. GRUENFELDER, JOHN K.
Gloucester's parliamentary elections 1604–40. *Bristol and Gloucestershire Arch. Soc. Trans.,* 98, 1979, p53–9.

331. H.O.P.T.
1509–1558 I, p95–6
1558–1603 I, p164–5
1660–1690 I, p241–3
1715–1754 I, p246–7
1754–1790 I, p290–2
1790–1820 II, p174–7

332. POWELL, J.J.
Members for Gloucester. *Gloucestriana,* (3304) Jan 1863, p85−130.

> Covers 1295 to 1800.

TEWKESBURY

See 2−3, 6, 16, 20−1, 26, 29−30, 35, 39−40, 308, 310.

333. BENNETT, JAMES.
The history of Tewkesbury. Tewkesbury: the author, 1830.

> Ch.XIX: Representatives in Parliament. Covers 1609−1832, mainly focussing on the Members. Appendix 34 reports an election petition in 1797. Appendix 35 concerns James Martin, MP.

334. H.O.P.T.
1660−1690 I, p243−4
1715−1754 I, p247−8
1754−1790 I, p292
1790−1820 II, p177−9

335. NOTES on old Tewkesbury past and present. Tewkesbury W. North, n.d.

> Brief section entitled: Tewkesbury for nearly three centuries a Parliamentary Borough, p6.

336. TEWKESBURY Members of Parliament. *Gloucestershire Notes and Queries* (ix), 1902 p90−6.

337. V.C.H. GLOUCESTERSHIRE
Vol VII, 1968 p153−4.

HAMPSHIRE

See 2−3, 6, 20−1, 26, 30, 35, 38−9.

338. BLACK, *Sir* FREDERICK.
An outline sketch of the parliamentary history of the Isle of Wight. Newport: County Press, 1929.

> Includes details of the constituencies of Newport, Newtown and Yarmouth as well as the county of Isle of Wight (created 1832).

339. FAITHFULL, WILLIAM.
The late Hampshire election. Winchester: the author, 1791.

> Refers to 1790.

340. FRITZE, R.H.
The role of family and religion in the local politics of early Elizabethan England: the case of Hampshire in the 1560s. *Hist. J.* 25, 1982 p267−87.

> Refers to the county only.

341. H.O.P.T.
      1509–1558 I, p97–8
      1558–1603 I, p165–7
      1660–1690 I, p244–5
      1715–1754 I, p248
      1754–1790 I, p292–3
      1790–1820 II, p179–82

342. LEGGE, HENRY BILSON.
Account of the character of, with letters and particulars relating to the Hampshire Election, 1759. 1764.

343. V.C.H. HAMPSHIRE
      Vol V, 1912 p293–358.

      References to parliamentary representation very brief.

ALRESFORD

See **343.**

344. V.C.H. HAMPSHIRE
      Vol III, 1908 p351.

ALTON

See **343.**

345. V.C.H. HAMPSHIRE
      Vol II, 1903 p479.

ANDOVER

See **2–3, 6, 20–1, 26, 30, 35, 39–40, 343.**

346. BUXTON, F.W.
Members of Parliament for Andover, from 1295 to 1880. 1881.

347. H.O.P.T.
      1558–1603 I, p167–8
      1660–1690 I, p245–7
      1715–1754 I, p248–9
      1754–1790 I, p293–4
      1790–1820 II, p182–3

348. JONES, R. ARNOLD.
Members of Parliament for Andover, 1295–1885. Andover: Andover Local Archives Committee, 1972.

      Good piece of local history. Includes alphabetical and chronological lists of Members.

349. V.C.H. HAMPSHIRE
      Vol IV, 1911 p351.

BASINGSTOKE
See **3, 343.**

350. BAIGENT, FRANCIS JOSEPH.
A history of the ancient town and manor of Basingstoke in the county of Southampton ... by Francis Joseph Baigent and James Elwin Millard. Basingstoke: C.J. Jacob, 1889.

> Very brief note giving known names of Members returned, 1295, 1302 and 1306 (p77).

351. V.C.H. HAMPSHIRE
Vol IV, 1911 p133.

CHRISTCHURCH
See **2−3, 6, 20−1, 26, 30, 35, 39−40, 343.**

352. H.O.P.T.
1558−1603 I, p168−9
1660−1690 I, p247−8
1715−1754 I, p249−50
1754−1790 I, p294
1790−1820 II, p183−5

353. LAVENDER, RUTH.
From pocket borough to parliamentary democracy: Christchurch 1572−1900. Dorset County Council Education Committee, 1976.

354. V.C.H. HAMPSHIRE
Vol V, 1912 p87.

FAREHAM
See **343.**

354. V.C.H. HAMPSHIRE
Vol III, 1908 p211.

LYMINGTON
See **2−3, 6, 20−1, 26, 30, 35−6, 39−40, 343.**

355. BURRARD, SIDNEY.
The annals of Walhampton. London: W.J. Johnson, 1874.

> Mostly concerned with the Burrard family. Many references to elections, especially in Chapters 2 and 5. No index.

356. H.O.P.T.
1558−1603 I, p169
1660−1690 I, p248−9
1715−1754 I, p250
1754−1790 I, p249−5
1790−1820 II, p185

357. KING, EDWARD.
Old times re-visited in the borough and parish of Lymington, Hants. Lymington: Charles T. King, 1900.

List of Members 1584–1895.

358. ST. BARBE, CHARLES.
Records of the Corporation of the Borough of New Lymington. London: Nichols & Son, 1848.

Lists Members from 1535 to 1831.

359. V.C.H. HAMPSHIRE
Vol IV, 1911 p641–2.

NEWPORT (IOW)

See **2–3, 6, 20, 22, 26, 30, 35, 37, 39, 338, 343.**

360. H.O.P.T.
1558–1603 I, p169
1669–1690 I, p249–50
1715–1754 I, p251
1754–1790 I, p295–6
1790–1820 II, p185–6

361. JAMES, EDWARD BOUCHER.
Letters archaeological and historical relating to the Isle of Wight. 2 vols. London: H. Frowde, 1896.

Vol I, p618–23: The parliamentary borough of Newport. Sections in Vol 2 relate to Newport elections in 1640, 1645 and 1706. Includes biographical details.

362. V.C.H. HAMPSHIRE
Vol V, 1912 p259.

NEWTOWN (IOW)

See **2–3, 6, 20, 26, 30, 35, 37, 39–40, 338, 343.**

363. H.O.P.T.
1558–1603 I, p169–70
1660–1690 I, p250–2
1715–1754 I, p251–2
1754–1790 I, p296
1790–1820 II, p186

364. V.C.H. HAMPSHIRE
Vol V, 1912 p265, 267.

OVERTON

O.R. only (Members first returned in 1295).

PETERSFIELD

See **2, 6, 10, 20–1, 26, 30, 35, 39–40, 343.**

365. H.O.P.T.
    1509–1558 I, p98–9
    1558–1603 I, p170
    1660–1690 I, p252–3
    1715–1754 I, p252
    1754–1790 I, p297
    1790–1820 II, p187

366. MINTY, E. ARDEN.
Some account of the history of Petersfield. London: John Lane, 1923.

    Discusses parliamentary representation briefly, and includes a list of MPs, 1307–1892. No index.

367. SURRY, NIGEL.
Petersfield and Parliament: one hundred years of a pocket borough 1685–1783. Petersfield: Petersfield Area Historical Society, 1983 (Petersfield Papers No.7).

    Illustrated. Includes a list of Members.

368. V.C.H. HAMPSHIRE
Vol III, 1908 p115–6.

PORCHESTER

O.R. only (Members returned on 3 January 1337).

PORTSMOUTH

See **2–3, 6, 20–1, 26, 30, 35–40, 343.**

369. GATES, WILLIAM G.
Illustrated history of Portsmouth. Portsmouth, Charpentier & Co., 1900.

    Ch.X. Covers 1298 to 1895, with some portraits.

370. H.O.P.T.
    1509–1558 I, p99–100
    1558–1603 I, p170–1
    1660–1690 I, p253–5
    1715–1754 I, p252–3
    1754–1790 I, p297–9
    1790–1820 II, p187–9

371. MURRELL, RICHARD J.
Extracts from records in the possession of the municipal corporation of the Borough of Portsmouth, by Richard J. Murrell and Robert East. Portsmouth: Henry Lewis, 1884.

    Lists Members from 1298–1835, with a list of additions.

372. V.C.H. HAMPSHIRE
Vol III, 1908 p184−5.

SOUTHAMPTON

See **2−3, 6−7, 20−1, 26, 30, 35, 37−40, 343.**

373. DAVIES, J. SILVESTER.
A history of Southampton. Southampton: Gilbert & Co., 1883.

Lists of MPs, 1295−1883, with brief biographical notes, p199−208.

374. H.O.P.T.
1509−1558 I, p100−2
1558−1603 I, p171−2
1660−1690 I, p255−6
1715−1754 I, p253−4
1754−1790 I, p299−301
1790−1820 II, p189−91

375. V.C.H. HAMPSHIRE
Vol III, 1908 p517−8.

STOCKBRIDGE

See **2−3, 6, 14, 20, 26, 30, 35, 39−40, 343.**

376. HILL, ROSALIND M.T.
The Stockbridge elections. *Hampshire Field Club Trans.,* XXIII, 1968 p120−7.

Covers 1563−1832.

377. H.O.P.T.
1558−1603 I, p172
1660−1690 I, p256−8
1715−1754 I, p254−5
1754−1790 I, p301
1790−1820 II, p191−3

378. V.C.H. HAMPSHIRE
Vol IV, 1911 p484.

WHITCHURCH

See **2−3, 6, 20, 26, 35, 39−40, 343.**

379. H.O.P.T.
1558−1603 I, p172−3
1660−1690 I, p258−9
1715−1754 I, p255−6
1754−1790 I, p301−2
1790−1820 II, p193

HAMPSHIRE

380. V.C.H. HAMPSHIRE
Vol IV, 1911 p301.

WINCHESTER

See **2−3, 6, 20, 26, 30, 35−6, 38−40, 343.**

381. ATKINSON, TOM.
Elizabethan Winchester. London: Faber & Faber, 1963.

Section on MPs in Ch.V: City officers, includes a list of them from 1559−1601.

382. H.O.P.T.
1509−1558 I, p102−4
1558−1603 I, p173
1660−1690 I, p259−60
1715−1754 I, p256−7
1754−1790 I, p302
1790−1820 II, p193−5

383. V.C.H. HAMPSHIRE
Vol V, 1912 p25−6.

YARMOUTH (IOW)

See **2−3, 6, 20, 26, 30, 35, 37, 39−40, 338, 343.**

384. H.O.P.T.
1558−1603 I, p174
1660−1690 I, p260−1
1715−1754 I, p257
1754−1790 I, p302−3
1790−1820 II, p195−6

385. V.C.H. HAMPSHIRE
Vol V, 1912 p288.

HEREFORDSHIRE

See **2−3, 6, 20−1, 26, 29−30, 35, 38−9.**

386. H.O.P.T.
1509−1558 I, p104−5
1558−1603 I, p174−5
1660−1690 I, p261−3
1715−1754 I, p257−8
1754−1790 I, p303
1790−1820 II, p196−7

387. NOBLE, F.
Herefordshire and Simon de Montford: 1265. *Woolhope Naturalists Field Club Trans.* 38, 1965, p111−8.

388. V.C.H. HEREFORDSHIRE
Vol I, 1908 p347—405.

> Mainly 1660—1832, including references to all boroughs.

389. WILLIAMS, WILLIAM RETLAW.
The parliamentary history of the county of Hereford, including the city of Hereford and the boroughs of Leominster, Weobley, Bromyard, Ledbury and Ross, from the earliest times to the present day, 1213—1896 ... Brecknock: Edwin Davies & Bell, 1896.

> The standard source. Arranged in chronological order of the dates of elections, taken from the Official Return. Includes biographical information.

BROMYARD

See **388—9.**

HEREFORD

See **2—3, 6, 20—1, 26, 29—30, 35, 38—40, 388—9.**

390. DAVIES, GODFREY.
The election at Hereford in 1702. *Huntington Library Q.,* XII, 1949 p322—7.

391. H.O.P.T.
    1509—1558 I, p105—7
    1558—1603 I, p175—6
    1660—1690 I, p263—5
    1715—1754 I, p258—9
    1754—1790 I, p303—4
    1790—1820 II, p197—9

LEDBURY

See **388—9.**

LEOMINSTER

See **2—3, 6, 8, 19—21, 26, 29—30, 35, 38—40, 388—9.**

392. H.O.P.T.
    1509—1558 I, p107—8
    1558—1603 I, p176—7
    1660—1690 I, p265—6
    1715—1754 I, p259
    1754—1790 I, p304—5
    1790—1820 II, p199—201

393. TOWNSEND, GEORGE FYLER.
The town and borough of Leominster: with illustrations of its ancient and modern history. Leominster: S. Partridge, 1863.

> Parliamentary history, p332—8, includes a list of Members from 1553 to 1859.

ROSS

See **388−9.**

WEOBLEY

See **2−3, 6, 20, 26, 30, 35, 39−40, 388−9.**

394. HILLABY, JOSEPH.
The parliamentary borough of Weobley, 1628−1708. *Woolhope Naturalists Field Club Trans.,* XXXIX, 1967 p104−51.

395. H.O.P.T.
1660−1690 I, p266−8
1715−1754 I, p259−60
1754−1790 I, p305
1790−1820 II, p201

396. SALT, A.E.W.
The borough and honour of Weobley. Hereford: Jakemans, 1954.

    Ch. 5: The parliamentary borough of Weobley, gives an interesting survey.

397. SCHAFER, R.G.
Robert Harley and the Weobley by-election of 1691. *Woolhope Naturalists Field Club Trans.,* 39, 1969 p456−66.

HERTFORDSHIRE

See **2−3, 6, 19−21, 26, 30, 35, 38−9.**

398. HILL, C.J.
The 1805 by-election in Hertfordshire, by C.J. Hill and P.F. Hazell. *Hertfordshire Past and Present* 6, 1966, p16−18.

399. H.O.P.T.
1509−1558 I, p108−9
1558−1603 I, p177
1660−1690 I, p268−9
1715−1754 I, p260−1
1754−1790 I, p305−7
1790−1820 II, p201−4

400. MUNBY, LIONEL MAXWELL.
The county election of 1727. *Hertfordshire Past and Present,* 1, 1960 p18−26.

401. MUNBY, LIONEL MAXWELL.
The early history of parliamentary politics in Hertfordshire. *East Hertforshire Arch. Soc. Trans. for 1955−61,* 14, 1964 p72−3.

    County and St. Albans politics 1584−1666.

402. STONE, LAWRENCE.
Electoral influence of the second Earl of Salisbury, 1614–68. *E.H.R.*, 71, July 1956 p384–400.

On elections in Hertfordshire, and Old Sarum.

403. V.C.H. HERTFORDSHIRE
Vol II, 1908 p1–45.

Mainly pre-1832.

BERKHAMSTEAD

See **403.**

404. BIRTCHNELL, PERCY C.
A short history of Berkhamstead. Berkhamstead, Percy Birtchnell, 1960.

Parliamentary representation briefly mentioned p44.

BISHOP'S STORTFORD

See **404.**

405. V.C.H. HERTFORDSHIRE
Vol III, 1912 p293.

HERTFORD

See **2–3, 6, 14, 20–1, 26, 30, 35, 39–40, 403.**

406. H.O.P.T.
1660–1690 I, p270–1
1715–1754 I, p261
1754–1790 I, p307
1790–1820 II, p204–5

407. PETTMAN, J.C.
The Reform Bill and the Hertford elections: the election of 1830. *Hertfordshire Past and Present,* (13) 1973 p30–40.

408. PETTMAN, J.C.
The Reform Bill and the Hertford elections, 2: the election of 1831. *Hertfordshire Past and Present,* (14) 1974 p60–72.

409. TURNOR, LEWIS.
History of the ancient town and borough of Hertford. Hertford: St. Austin & Sons, 1830.

Ch.V: Representative history. Includes list of MPs, 1298–1826, with biographical details of MPs after 1624.

410. V.C.H. HERTFORSHIRE
Vol III, 1912 p498.

ST. ALBANS

See 2–3, 6, 20–1, 23, 26, 30, 35, 39–40, 401, 403.

411. H.O.P.T.
1509–1558 I, p109–10
1558–1603 I, p177–8
1660–1690 I, p271–2
1715–1754 I, p261–3
1754–1790 I, p307–10
1790–1820 II, p205–9

412. LANSBERRY, H.C.F.
A Whig inheritance. *B.I.H.R.,* XLI, 1968, p47–57.

Lord Spencer and St Albans 1768–1807.

413. PAGE, WILLIAM.
St Albans. London: Society for Promoting Christian Knowledge, 1920. (Story of the English Towns).

Ch.VIII: Political corruption, discusses elections in St Albans since 1628.

414. V.C.H. HERTFORDSHIRE
Vol II, 1908 p479, 482–3.

HUNTINGDONSHIRE

See 2–3, 6, 19–21, 26, 30, 34–5, 38–9.

415. H.O.P.T.
1509–1558 I, p110–1
1558–1603 I, p178–9
1660–1690 I, p272–3
1715–1754 I, p263–4
1754–1790 I, p310–1
1790–1820 II, p209–13

416. PROBY, GRANVILLE.
Huntingdonshire Members of Parliament, 1290–1945. *Cambridgeshire and Huntingdonshire Arch. Soc. Trans.,* VI, 1947 p215–43.

417. V.C.H. HUNTINGDONSHIRE
Vol II, 1932 p1–72.

Parliamentary history from sixteenth century to 1959 in a separate section. Includes references to borough representation.

HUNTINGDON

See 2–3, 6, 20–1, 26, 30, 35, 38–40, 417.

418. GRIFFITH, EDWARD.

A collection of ancient records relating to the borough of Huntingdon with observations illustrative of the history of parliamentary boroughs in general. London: Henry Butterworth, 1827.

Mainly concerned with Burgesses and their rights. More a commentary on documents than a history of representation. No index.

419. H.O.P.T.

1509–1558 I, p111–2
1558–1603 I, p179–80
1660–1690 I, p273–4
1715–1754 I, p264–5
1754–1790 I, p311–2
1790–1820 II, p213

420. V.C.H. HUNTINGDONSHIRE

Vol II, 1932 p134.

KENT

See 2–3, 6, 19–21, 26, 30, 35, 38–9.

421. CAVE-BROWN, JOHN.

Knights of the Shire for Kent, 1275–1831. *Archaeologia Cantiana,* XXI, 1895 p198–243.

422. CAVE-BROWN, JOHN.

Knights of the Shire for Kent from A.D. 1275 to A.D. 1831. Mitchell and Hughes, 1894.

423. CHALKLIN, C.W.

Seventeenth-century Kent: a social and economic history. London: Longmans, 1965.

Ch.XII: The gentry, contains references to the political leadership of the county.

424. CLARK, PETER.

English provincial society from the Reformation to the Revolution: religion, politics and society in Kent 1500–1640. Hassocks: Harvester Press, 1977.

Concentrates on the county but includes references to Canterbury, Maidstone, Queenborough, Rochester and the Cinque Ports: Dover, Hythe, New Romney and Sandwich.

425. EVERITT, ALAN.

The community of Kent and the Great Rebellion 1640–60. Leicester: Leicester U.P., 1966.

The elections of 1640, p69–83. Also many references to parliament and elections in the index.

426. FURLEY, ROBERT.

A history of the Weald of Kent, with an outline of the history of the county to the present time 2 vols in 3 parts. Ashford: Henry Igglesden, 1874.

Lists Knights of the Shire during the reign of Edward II, in alphabetical order, Vol 2 i p306–7. Section on the elective franchise including a chronological list of MPs for Kent 1800–1868, Vol 2 ii p684–9.

427. HASTED, EDWARD.

The history and topographical survey of the county of Kent ... 4 vols. Canterbury: Simmons & Kirkby, 1778–1799.

Includes brief accounts of parliamentary representation, with list of Members, for the county and the boroughs of Canterbury, Dover, Hythe, Maidstone, New Romney, Queenborough, Rochester and Sandwich.

428. H.O.P.T.

1509–1558 I, p112–4
1558–1603 I, p180–3
1660–1690 I, p274–6
1715–1754 I, p265
1754–1790 I, p312–3
1790–1820 II, p214–5

429. JESSUP, FRANK W.

The Kentish election of March, 1640. *Archaeologia Cantiana,* 86, 1971 p1–10.

430. LANDAU, NORMA.

Independence, deference and voter participation: the behaviour of the electorate in early eighteenth century Kent. *Hist. J.,* 22, 1979 p561–83.

Concentrates on the county, but also mentions Dover, Hythe, New Romney, Queenborough and Rochester.

431. V.C.H. KENT

Vol III, 1932 p271–317.

Not covered in detail. Includes brief references to boroughs.

CANTERBURY

See **2–3, 6–7, 20–1, 23, 26, 30, 35, 38–40, 424, 427, 431, 758.**

432. BRENT, JOHN.

Canterbury in the olden time. 2nd ed. Canterbury: Simpkin, Marshall & Co, 1879.

Chapter on Representatives in Parliament p78–82. Covers up to 1661.

433. H.O.P.T.

1509–1558 I, p114–6
1558–1603 I, p183–4
1660–1690 I, p276–7
1715–1754 I, p265–6
1754–1790 I, p313
1790–1820 II, p215–7

DOVER

See **960–1.**

FAVERSHAM

See **Cinque Ports.**

HYTHE

See **967–8.**

MAIDSTONE

See **2–3, 6, 20–1, 23, 26, 30, 32, 35, 39–40, 424, 427, 431.**

434. H.O.P.T.
1509–1558 I, p116–7
1558–1603 I, p184–5
1660–1690 I, p278–9
1715–1754 I, p266–7
1754–1790 I, p313–4
1790–1820 II, p217–8

435. Russell, J.M.
The History of Maidstone. Maidstone: William S. Vivish, 1881.

> Ch.9: Municipal and parliamentary history. Appendix 1 gives a list of MPs, 1562–1880.

NEW ROMNEY

See **969–70.**

QUEENBOROUGH

See **2–3, 6, 20, 26, 30, 35, 37, 40, 424, 427, 430–1.**

436. H.O.P.T.
1558–1603 I, p185
1660–1690 I, p279–80
1715–1754 I, p267–8
1754–1790 I, p314
1790–1820 II, p218–20

ROCHESTER

See **2–3, 6, 8, 20–1, 26, 30, 35, 37–40, 424, 427, 430–1.**

437. H.O.P.T.
1509–1558 I, p117–8
1558–1603 I, p185–6
1660–1690 I, p280–2
1715–1754 I, p268
1754–1790 I, p314–5
1790–1820 II, p220–2

438. SMITH, FREDERICK FRANCIS.
A history of Rochester. London: C.W. Daniel Co., 1928.

> Ch.XVIII: Parliamentary representation. Appendix lists MPs, 1295–1924, with brief notes.

439. SMITH, FREDERICK FRANCIS.
Rochester in Parliament 1295–1933, including the Chatham and Gillingham Divisions of Rochester, also the Borough of Chatham from June 1832 to 1918. London: Simpkin Marshall & Co., 1933.

> Includes a list of Members elected in chronological order, followed by brief biographies of each.

SANDWICH

See **975–6.**

TUNBRIDGE

See **431.**

LANCASHIRE

See **1–3, 6, 20–1, 24, 26, 30, 35–6, 38–9.**

440. BAINES, EDWARD.
The history of the County Palatine and Duchy of Lancaster. New revised and enlarged edn. 4 vols. Manchester: John Heywood, 1888.

> Vol.1 Ch.VIII: Representative history of the county. Also covers the boroughs, which are mentioned separately in later volumes.

441. BAINES, THOMAS.
Lancashire and Cheshire, past and present: history and description of the palatine counties of Lancaster and Chester. 2 vols. London: William Mackenzie, 1868–9.

> Discusses the progress of the parliamentary and municipal boroughs: vol. 1 p635–7, vol.2 Chapter III, p440–60.

442. FISHWICK, HENRY.
A history of Lancashire. London: Elliot Stock, 1894. (Popular County Histories).

> Refers to the parliamentary representation of the county and each of its boroughs.

443. H.O.P.T.
1509–1558 I, p118–20
1558–1603 I, p186–7
1660–1690 I, p282–4
1715–1754 I, p268–9
1754–1790 I, p315
1790–1820 II, p222–3

444. HORNYOLD-STRICKLAND, HENRY.
Biographical sketches of the Members of Parliament of Lancashire (1290–1550). Manchester: Chetham Society, 1935.

> Also covers Members elected for the Boroughs of Lancaster, Preston, Liverpool and Wigan.

445. ORMEROD, FRANK.
Lancashire life and character, 2nd ed. Rochdale: Edwards & Bryning, 1915.

> Ch.VIII: Election humour.

446. PINK, W. DUNCOMBE.
The parliamentary representation of Lancashire (County and Borough), 1258–1885, by W. Duncombe Pink and the Rev Alfred B. Beavan. London: Henry Gray, 1889.

> Includes biographical and genealogical notices of each Member. Entries are arranged in chronological order of election.

447. ROSKELL, JOHN SMITH.
The Knights of the Shire for the County Palatine of Lancaster, 1377–1460. Manchester: Chetham Society, 1937. (Vol 96 — new series).

> Extensive biographies for each Member elected during the period, as well as background chapters.

448. SOMERVILLE, ROBERT.
History of the Duchy of Lancaster. London: Duchy of Lancaster, 1953. (Vol 1, 1265–1603).

> Includes references to parliamentary representation.

449. V.C.H. LANCASHIRE
Vol II, 1908 p178–259.

> Mentions Lancaster, Preston, Wigan, Liverpool, Newton and Clitheroe, but only briefly. Nineteenth century covered in more detail.

450. WILLIAMS, WILLIAM RETLAW.
Official lists of the Duchy and County Palatine of Lancaster from earliest times to the present day. Brecknock (?): the author, 1901.

> Includes a list of Chancellors of the Duchy of Lancaster, many of whom were MPs. Name index.

CLITHEROE

See **1–3, 6, 20–1, 26, 30, 35, 39–40, 440, 442, 449.**

451. H.O.P.T.
1558–1603 I, p187–8
1660–1690 I, p284–6
1715–1754 I, p269
1754–1790 I, p316
1790–1820 II, p223–4

452. V.C.H. LANCASHIRE
Vol VI, 1911 p368.

LANCASTER

See **1−3, 6, 8, 20−1, 26, 30, 35, 39−40, 440, 442, 444, 446, 449.**

453. H.O.P.T.
1509−1558 I, p120−2
1558−1603 I, p188−9
1660−1690 I, p286−8
1715−1754 I, p270
1754−1790 I, p316−7
1790−1820 II, p224−8

454. SIMPSON, ROBERT.
The history and antiquities of the town of Lancaster. Lancaster: T. Edmondson, 1852.

Parliamentary history p322−7, includes a list of Members 1295−1848.

LIVERPOOL

See **1−3, 6, 19−21, 26, 30, 35, 39−40, 440, 442, 444, 449.**

455. H.O.P.T.
1509−1558 I, p122−4
1558−1603 I, p189−90
1660−1690 I, p288−90
1715−1754 I, p270−2
1754−1790 I, p317−8
1790−1820 II, p228−34

456. MATHEWS, GODFREY W.
Some notes on the Liverpool election of 1806. *Historic Soc. of Lancashire and Cheshire Trans.*, 79, 1928 p75−85.

457. MENZIES, E.M.
The freeman voter in Liverpool, 1802−1835. *Historic Soc. of Lancashire and Cheshire Trans.*, 124, 1972 p85−107.

458. MUIR, RAMSAY.
A history of Liverpool. Liverpool: L.U.P., 1907.

Scattered references to parliamentary representation.

459. TOUZEAU, JAMES.
The rise and progress of Liverpool from 1551 to 1835. Liverpool: Liverpool Booksellers Company, 1910.

Material from the Corporation records. References in the index to MPs and elections.

460. V.C.H. LANCASHIRE
Vol IV, 1911 p5, 19.

MANCHESTER

See **1, 21, 30, 442.**

461. AXON, WILLIAM E.A.
The annals of Manchester: a chronological record from the earliest times to the end of 1885. Manchester: John Heywood, 1886.

Brief references made to pre-1832 representation.

462. COURT Leet records of the manor of Manchester from the year 1552 to the year 1686, and from the year 1731 to the year 1846. 12 vols. Manchester: Henry Blacklock & Co., 1884–90.

Vol 4, 1647 to 1662 contains the records relating to the first Member returned in 1654.

463. SAINTSBURY, GEORGE.
Manchester. London: Longmans, Green & Co., 1887.

Ch.5: Military and political importance of Manchester, mentions parliamentary representation.

464. V.C.H. LANCASHIRE
Vol IV, 1911 p235.

NEWTON

See **1–3, 6, 20, 26, 30, 35, 39–40, 440, 442, 449.**

465. ANDERTON, H.I.
Robert Langton, MP for Newton in Makerfield, 1584–5, 1586–7, 1588–9 and 1593. *Notes and Queries,* CLXIX, 1935 p186–8.

466. H.O.P.T.
1558–1603 I, p190
1660–1690 I, p290–1
1715–1754 I, p272
1754–1790 I, p318
1790–1820 II, p234–5

467. V.C.H. LANCASHIRE
Vol IV, 1911 p132, 135.

PRESTON

See **1–3, 6, 20–2, 26, 30, 35, 37, 39–40, 440, 442, 444, 449.**

468. CLEMESHA, H.W.
A history of Preston in Amounderness. Manchester: M.U.P., 1912.

Ch.VIII covers political history after 1800. Many references to parliamentary representation in the index.

469. DOBSON, WILLIAM.
History of the parliamentary representation of Preston. 2nd ed. Preston:
W. & J. Dobson, 1868.

A narrative covering representation up to 1865, with a note of the 1868 General
Election. No index.

470. FISHWICK, HENRY.
The history of the parish of Preston, in Amounderness in the county of
Lancaster. Rochdale: James Clegg, 1900.

Ch.XV: Members from 1297–1895, with biographical notes.

471. FLINTOFF, THOMAS R.
Preston and Parliament: a review of some interesting events. Preston:
T.R. Flintoff, 1980.

Covers the period 1295 to 1979, but concentrates mainly on the twentieth
century. Includes many portraits.

472. H.O.P.T.
1509–1558 I, p124–6
1558–1603 I, p190–1
1660–1690 I, p291–3
1715–1754 I, p272–4
1754–1790 I, p319
1790–1820 II, p235–8

473. PROCTOR, WINIFRED.
The Preston election of 1768. (Electioneering in Lancashire before the
secret ballot — 1.) *Historic Soc. of Lancashire and Chesire Trans.,* (111)
1959 p93–166.

474. V.C.H. LANCASHIRE
Vol VIII, 1912 p72, 78.

475. WHITTLE, P.
A topographical, statistical and historical account of the borough of
Preston ..., by Marmaduke Tulket (i.e. P. Whittle). Preston: the
author, 1821.

Preston representative history, p252–62, includes a list of MPs, 1295–1820
and an interesting description of the practice of "chairing" the newly elected
MPs.

WIGAN
See **1–3, 6, 20–1, 26, 30, 35, 39–40, 440, 442, 444, 449.**

476. COX, MARJORIE.
Sir Roger Bradshaigh and the electoral management of Wigan
1695–1747. *B. of John Rylands Library,* 37, (1), 1954. p120–64.

477. H.O.P.T.
1509–1558 I, p126–8
1558–1603 I, p191–2
1660–1690 I, p293–4
1715–1754 I, p274
1754–1790 I, p319–22
1790–1820 II, p238–40

478. V.C.H. LANCASHIRE
Vol IV, 1911 p74.

LEICESTERSHIRE
See **2–3, 6, 20–1, 26, 30, 35, 38–9.**

479. CURTIS, J.
A topographical history of the county of Leicester. Ashby-de-la-Zouch: W. Hextall, 1831.

Members 1294–1831 listed in the Introduction, with notes on some of the elections. (p. xxiii–xxvii).

480. H.O.P.T.
1509–1558 I, p128–9
1558–1603 I, p192–3
1660–1690 I, p295–6
1715–1754 I, p274–5
1754–1790 I, p322
1790–1820 II, p240–1

481. V.C.H. LEICESTERSHIRE
Vol II, 1954 p74–144.

Divided into periods. Medieval section concentrates on the county; 1530–1885 includes discussion of borough elections.

LEICESTER
See **2–3, 6, 19–21, 26, 35, 38–40.**

482. BENNETT, J.D.
Members of Parliament for Leicester 1832–1983 (with an appendix of MPs 1294–1832). Leicester: Chamberlain Music & Books, 1984.

No biographical details of pre 1832 MPs.

483. GREAVES, ROBERT WILLIAM.
The corporation of Leicester 1689–1836. Oxford: O.U.P., 1939.

Index contains references to the franchise and individual parliamentary elections.

484. GREAVES, ROBERT WILLIAM.
Roman Catholic relief and the Leicester election of 1826. *Royal Hist. Soc. Trans.,* 4th Series XXII, 1940 p199–223.

485. H.O.P.T.
1509–1558 I, p129–31
1558–1603 I, p193–5
1660–1690 I, p296–8
1715–1754 I, p275–6
1754–1790 I, p322–4
1790–1820 II, p241–3

486. PATTERSON, A. TEMPLE.
Radical Leicester: a history of Leicester 1780–1850. Leicester: University College, 1954.

Especially Ch.4: Leicester politics and the French Revolution 1789–96; Ch.8: The election of 1826; and Ch.10: The parliamentary reform struggle, 1830–2.

487. READ, ROBERT, *Junior*.
Modern Leicester: jottings of personal experience and research ... London: Simpkin, Marshall & Co., 1881.

A contemporary account of the contested election in 1826, p221–48.

488. RECORDS OF THE BOROUGH OF LEICESTER: being a series of extracts from the archives of the Corporation of Leicester.
Vol 1, 1103–1327; edited by Mary Bateson. London: C.J. Clay, 1899. (MPs 1295–1327, p404).
Vol 2, 1327–1509; edited by Mary Bateson. London: C.J. Clay, 1901. (MPs 1327–1504, p460–2).
Vol 3, 1509–1603; edited by Mary Bateson. Cambridge: C.U.P., 1905. (MPs 1523–160I, p460).
Vol 4, 1603–1688; edited by Helen Stocks. Cambridge: C.U.P., 1923. (MPs 1604–1688, p599–600).
Vol 5, Hall books and papers 1689–1835; edited by G.A. Chinnery. Leicester: L.U.P., 1965. (MPs who served 1688–1835, p518).
Vol 6, The Chamberlains' accounts 1688–1835; edited by G.A. Chinnery. Leicester: L.U.P., 1967.

All the above volumes contain references to elections.

489. SIMMONS, JACK.
Leicester past and present. 2 Vols. London: Eyre Methuen, 1974.

Vol 1 Ancient borough to 1860. References best picked out from the index.

490. V.C.H. LEICESTERSHIRE
Vol IV, 1958 p110–52.

Parliamentary history divided into periods. Good index.

LINCOLNSHIRE

See **2–3, 6, 19–21, 26, 30, 35, 38–9.**

491. H.O.P.T.
1509–1558 I, p131–3
1558–1603 I, p195
1660–1690 I, p298–9
1715–1754 I, p276–7
1754–1790 I, p324
1790–1820 II, p243–5

492. OLNEY, R.J.
Rural society and county government in nineteenth century Lincolnshire. Lincoln: History of Lincolnshire Committee, 1979. (History of Lincolnshire, 10).

Ch.8: Party politics, discusses the pre-reform situation in the county.

493. ROGERS, ALAN.
Parliamentary electors in Lincolnshire in the fifteenth century. *Lincolnshire History and Archaeology* (4) 1969, p33−53; (5) 1970, p47−58; (6) 1971, p67, 81.

494. ROSKELL, JOHN SMITH.
The parliamentary representation of Lincolnshire during the reigns of Richard II, Henry IV and Henry V. *Nottingham Medieval Studies,* Vol III, 1959 p53−77.

Covers 1377 to 1422, and includes a list of Lincolnshire Knights of the Shire in addition to discussing them extensively in the text. Detailed footnotes. Reprinted in J.S. Roskell. *Parliament and politics in late medieval England.* 3 vols. Hambledon Press, 1981 (Vol 1).

495. V.C.H. LINCOLNSHIRE
Vol II, 1906 p245−92.

Includes references to borough representation. Some details of prominent families, but treatment generally brief.

BOSTON

See 2−3, 6, 20−1, 26, 29−30, 35, 39−40, 495.

496. H.O.P.T.
1509−1558 I, p133
1558−1603 I, p195−6
1660−1690 I, p299−300
1715−1754 I, p277
1754−1790 I, p324−5
1790−1820 II, p245−7

497. THOMPSON, PISHEY.
The history and antiquities of Boston ... Boston: John Noble, Jun., 1856.

Members of Parliament 1352−1856, with biographical notes, p499−53.

GRANTHAM

See 2−3, 6, 20−1, 26, 30, 35, 38−40, 495.

498. DAVIES, GODFREY.
The by-election at Grantham, 1678. *Huntingdon Library Q.,* VII (2), 1944 p179−82.

499. H.O.P.T.
      1509−1558 I, p133−4
      1558−1603 I, p196−7
      1660−1690 I, p300−2
      1715−1754 I, p277−8
      1754−1790 I, p325−6
      1790−1820 II, p247−9

500. STREET, B.
Historical notes on Grantham and Grantham Church. Grantham: S. Ridge & Son, 1857.

Members for the Borough, p115. Brief.

501. TURNOR, EDMUND.
Collections for the history of the town and soke of Grantham. London: William Miller, 1806.

Gives list of burgesses from 1467−1802, with brief biographical notes p56−9.

GRIMSBY

See **2−3, 6, 19−21, 26, 29−30, 35, 38−40, 495.**

502. BATES, ANDERSON.
A gossip about old Grimsby. Grimsby: Albert Gait, 1893.

Section on Elections, p53−66. An appendix lists Grimsby elections, 1639−1893.

503. GILLETT, EDWARD.
A history of Grimsby. London: O.U.P., 1970.

Ch.X: The Parliamentary Borough 1688−1782; Ch.XII: The French War and the growth of the town; Appendix I: Early parliamentary history; other scattered references. Well researched.

504. H.O.P.T.
      1509−1558 I, p134−6
      1558−1603 I, p197−8
      1660−1690 I, p302−4
      1715−1754 I, p278
      1754−1790 I, p326−7
      1790−1820 II, p249−53.

505. OLIVER, GEORGE.
The monumental antiquities of Great Grimsby. Hull: Isaac Wilson, 1825.

Ch. IV, p114−23, consists of a list of MPs from 1295 to 1823.

506. ROGERS, ALAN.
Parliamentary elections in Grimsby in the fifteenth century. *B.I.H.R.,* XLII, 1969 p212−20.

Refers to 1447, 1455, 1460, 1463, 1483 and 1487.

LINCOLN

See **2−3, 6−7, 20−1, 26, 30, 35, 38−40, 495.**

507. HILL, JAMES W.F.
Georgian Lincoln. Cambridge: C.U.P., 1966.

> Ch.4: Patronage and parliamentary representation. Covers the eighteenth century.

508. HILL, JAMES W.F.
Tudor and Stuart Lincoln. Cambridge: C.U.P., 1956.

> Many references to parliamentary representation in index.

509. H.O.P.T.
1509−1558 I, p136−7
1558−1603 I, p198−9
1660−1690 I, p304−5
1715−1754 I, p278−8
1754−1790 I, p327−8
1790−1820 II, p253−5

LOUTH

See **495.**

STAMFORD

See **2−3, 6, 20−1, 26, 30, 35, 38−40, 495.**

510. DRAKARD, JOHN.
The history of Stamford in the county of Lincoln. Stamford: the author, 1822.

> Ch.V: State of the representation, includes a list of MPs from 1295 to 1820, but based on unreliable sources.

511. H.O.P.T.
1509−1558 I, p137−9
1558−1603 I, p199−200
1660−1690 I, p305−8
1715−1754 I, p279
1754−1790 I, p328−9
1790−1820 II, p255−8

512. ROGERS, ALAN.
The making of Stamford; edited by Alan Rogers. Leicester: L.U.P., 1965.

> Brief references to parliamentary representation, some of which are post-1832.

MIDDLESEX

See **2, 6, 14−15, 19−21, 26, 29−30, 35, 38−9.**

513. BANKS, C. O.
List of the Middlesex knights of the shire from 1295–1832: extracts from the Parliamentary Returns and Sir Richard de Wyndesore, of Stanwell, Middlesex. *London and Middlesex Arch. Soc. Trans.*, New Series VI (II), 1930? p343–69.

514. HISTORY of the Westminster and Middlesex elections in the month of November 1806. London: Budd, Bagshaw & Humphrey, 1807.

Detailed account of one particular campaign. No index.

515. H.O.P.T.
1509–1558 I, p145–6
1558–1603 I, p200
1660–1690 I, p308–10
1715–1754 I, p283–5
1754–1790 I, p331–5
1790–1820 II, p258–63

516. RUDE, GEORGE.
The Middlesex electors of 1768–1769. *E.H.R.*, 75, 1960 p601–17.

517. RUDE, GEORGE.
John Wilkes and the Middlesex election. *History Today,* XI, 1961 p128–35.

518. V.C.H. MIDDLESEX
Vol II, 1911 p15–60.

Discusses parliamentary representation separately (county only).

LONDON

See **2–3, 6–7, 20–1, 26, 29–30, 35, 38–40.**

519. BEAVEN, ALFRED B.
The aldermen of the City of London; with notes on the parliamentary representation of the city ... etc. London: Fisher & Co., 1908.

Includes a list of Members from 1283–1908, which updates and corrects the Official Return. Brief biographical notes are given. There is also a list of Aldermen who were elected to Parliament for constituencies other than the City of London.

520. DAVIS, ELIZA JEFFRIES.
A parliamentary election in 1298. *B.I.H.R.,* III, 1925–6 p45–6.

Note of a return for London.

521. H.O.P.T.
1509–1558 I, p139–43
1558–1603 I, p200–2
1660–1690 I, p310–5
1715–1754 I, p279–83
1754–1790 I, p329–30
1790–1820 II, p263–6

522. McKisack, May.
Borough representation in Richard II's reign. *E.H.R.*, XXXIX, 1924 p511–25.

> Although a general survey, includes a substantial discussion of London representatives.

523. Miller, Helen.
London and Parliament in the reign of Henry VIII. *B.I.H.R.*, 35, November 1962, p128–49.

> Concentrates more on the administration of the City of London than on its representatives in Parliament.

524. Noorthouck, John.
A new history of London including Westminster and Southwark. London: R. Baldwin, 1773.

> Contains a list of London MPs, 1298–1768.

525. Speck, William A.
Londoners at the polls under Anne and George I, by W.A. Speck and W.A. Gray. *Guildhall Studies in London History,* 1, Apr.1975 p253–62.

> Covers 1710–1722.

WESTMINSTER

See **2–3, 6, 10, 15, 19–21, 26, 30, 35, 37, 39–40, 514.**

526. Aspinall, Arthur.
The Westminster election of 1814. *E.H.R.*, XL, 1925 p562–9.

527. H.O.P.T.
    1509–1558 I, p143–5
    1558–1603 I, p202–3
    1660–1690 I, p315–7
    1715–1754 I, p285–8
    1754–1790 I, p335–7
    1790–1820 II, p266–83

528. Laprade, William Thomas.
William Pitt and Westminster elections. *American Hist. R.*, XVIII, 1913 p253–74.

> Refers to 1784 and 1788.

529. Mayhew, George.
Swift's political 'conversion' and his 'lost' ballad on the Westminster election of 1710. *B. of John Rylands Library,* 53, Spring 1971 p397–427.

MONMOUTHSHIRE

See 2, 6, 20–1, 26, 30, 35, 39–40.

530. H.O.P.T.
    1509–1558 I, p146–7
    1558–1603 I, p203–5
    1660–1690 I, p317–8
    1715–1754 I, p288
    1754–1790 I, p338
    1790–1820 II, p283

531. NEALE, *Sir* JOHN ERNEST.
More Elizabethan elections. *E.H.R.* , LXI, 1946 p18–44.

    Refers to Haverfordwest, 1571; Monmouthshire, 1601 and Rutland, 1601.

532. WILLIAMS, WILLIAM RETLAW.
Parliamentary representation of the principality of Wales, from the earliest times to the present day, 1541–1895. Brecknock: privately printed for the author by Edwin Davies & Bell, 1895.

    Monmouthshire p120–33; Monmouth p133–41. Written in the same format and style as his other works, with an index of Members and defeated candidates.

MONMOUTH

See 2, 6, 14, 20–1, 26, 30, 35, 39–40.

533. H.O.P.T.
    1509–1558 I, p147–8
    1558–1603 I, p205–6
    1660–1690 I, p318–9
    1715–1754 I, p288–9
    1754–1790 I, p338
    1790–1820 II, p283–4

NORFOLK

See 2–3, 6, 13–14, 19–21, 26, 30, 35, 38–9.

534. ALSOP, J.D.
Contemporary remarks on the 1768 election in Norfolk and Suffolk. *Norfolk Archaeology*, 38, 1981 p79–82.

535. ARMSTRONG, MOSTYN JOHN.
History and antiquities of the county of Norfolk. 10 vols. Norwich: J. Crouse, 1781.

    Lists Knights of the Shire for Norfolk, 1708–1780, Vol 1 p40–43. Mentions all boroughs, and gives the Members for each in 1780. No index.

536. CHAMBERS, JOHN.
General history of the county of Norfolk, intended to convey all the information of a Norfolk tour. 2 vols. Norwich: John Stacy, 1829.

Includes lists of MPs for the county (1660–1826); Great Yarmouth (1660–1820); Norwich (1660–1826); Lynn (1430–1450). Biographies of prominent persons in each locality may include MPs.

537. HAYTON, DAVID.
A note on the Norfolk election of 1702. *Norfolk Archaeology* (37) 1980, p320–4.

538. H.O.P.T.
1509–1558 I, p148–9
1558–1603 I, p206–10
1660–1690 I, p319–22
1715–1754 I, p289
1754–1790 I, p339
1790–1820 II, p284–7

539. LE STRANGE, HAMON.
Norfolk official lists, from the earliest period to the present day. Norwich: Agas Goose, 1890.

Includes lists of Members of Parliament for the county and Castle Rising, Lynn, Norwich, Thetford and Yarmouth. Some names supplement the Official Return.

540. McFARLANE, K.B.
Parliament and bastard feudalism. *Royal Hist. Soc. Trans.*, 4th series XXVI, 1944 p53–79.

Based on the Paston letters. Discusses several Norfolk elections of the late 15th century.

541. MACKIE, CHARLES.
Norfolk annals: a chronological record of remarkable events in the nineteenth century, compiled from the files of the Norfolk Chronicle. 2 vols. Norwich: Norfolk Chronicle, 1901.

Vol 1, 1801–1850 includes references to parliamentary elections in the index. Brief references in the text to elections for the county and the boroughs.

542. MASON, R. HINDRY.
The history of Norfolk. Part 1: General history of the county. London: Wertheimer, Lea & Co, 1884.

Lists Knights of the Shire for short periods at various points throughout the volume. No index.

543. SMITH, ALFRED HASSELL.
County and court: government and politics in Norfolk 1558–1603. Oxford: Clarendon Press, 1974.

Mentions all boroughs. Consult the index under the name of the county and of each borough.

544. V.C.H. NORFOLK
   Vol II, 1906 p467–527.

   References brief, mainly 17th and 18th centuries. Boroughs mentioned.

545. WILLIAMS, CHARLES H.
   A Norfolk parliamentary election, 1461. *E.H.R.*, XL, 1925 p79–86.

CASTLE RISING

See **2–3, 6, 20, 26, 30, 35, 39–40, 539, 541, 543–4.**

546. BRADFER-LAWRENCE, H.L.
   Castle Rising and the Walpoles. in: *Supplement to Blomefield's Norfolk;*
   ed. Clement Ingleby. London: the author, 1929 p29–46.

   Covers 1558–1722, with extracts from contemporary records.

547. H.O.P.T.
   1509–1558 I, p149
   1558–1603 I, p210–1
   1660–1690 I, p323–4
   1715–1754 I, p289–90
   1754–1790 I, p339–40
   1790–1820 II, p287–9

GREAT YARMOUTH

See **2–3, 6, 20–1, 26, 30, 35, 38–40, 536, 539, 541, 543–4.**

548. CHRISTIE, IAN R.
   Great Yarmouth and the Yorkshire Reform Movement, 1782–1784.
   Norfolk Archaeology, 32, 1961 p104–10. Reprinted in his *Myth and
   reality in late eighteenth century British politics.* London: Macmillan,
   1970.

549. DRUERY, JOHN HENRY.
   Historical and topographical notices of Great Yarmouth in Norfolk ...
   London: Nichols & Son, 1826.

   Parliamentary representation discussed, p344–56, including a list of MPs,
   1299–1826.

550. H.O.P.T.
   1509–1558 I, p149–50
   1558–1603 I, p211–2
   1660–1690 I, p324–7
   1715–1754 I, p290
   1754–1790 I, p340–1
   1790–1820 II, p289–92

551. NALL, JOHN GREAVES.
   Great Yarmouth and Lowestoft: a handbook for visitors and residents
   ... London: Longmans, Green, Reader & Dyer, 1866.

   Section called: Parliamentary notes, p107–10.

552. PALMER, CHARLES JOHN.
The history of Great Yarmouth. Great Yarmouth: Louis Alfred Meall, 1856.

Section V: Representation of the borough in Parliament. Includes lists of Members, 1308–1852, with biographical notes.

KING'S LYNN

See **2–3, 6, 20–1, 30, 35, 38–40, 536, 539, 541, 543–4.**

553. HILLEN, HENRY J.
History of the borough of King's Lynn. 2 vols. Norwich: East of England Newspaper Co., 1907.

Scattered references to parliamentary elections.

554. H.O.P.T.
1509–1558 I, p150–2
1558–1603 I, p212
1660–1690 I, p327–9
1715–1754 I, p290
1754–1790 I, p341
1790–1820 II, p292

555. McKISACK, MAY.
The parliamentary representation of King's Lynn before 1500. *E.H.R.*, XLII, 1927 p583–9.

556. WOOD, S.
Walpole's constituency: King's Lynn. *History Today*, 30, April 1980 p40–4.

Mainly a portrait of the port in the early eighteenth century.

NORWICH

See **2–3, 6–7, 20–2, 26, 30, 32, 35, 38–40, 536, 539, 541, 543–4.**

557. BAYNE, A. D.
A comprehensive history of Norwich ... London: Jarrold & Sons, 1869.

Part 4 covers political history. Incudes a list of Members, 1298–1869.

558. BLOMEFIELD, FRANCIS.
History of the city and county of Norwich. London: William Miller, 1806. (History of Norfolk, Vol III).

Chapters describe the city in each reign. A list of burgesses in Parliament is given at the end of each chapter.

559. EVANS, JOHN T.
Seventeenth century Norwich: politics, religion and government 1620–1690. Oxford: Clarendon Press, 1979.

Concentrates mainly on local government, but has some interesting details of local Members of Parliament.

560. H.O.P.T.
    1509–1558 I, p152–3
    1558–1603 I, p212–3
    1660–1690 I, p329–32
    1715–1754 I, p291
    1754–1790 I, p342
    1790–1820 II, p292–5

561. Jewson, Charles B.
The Jacobin city: a portrait of Norwich in its reaction to the French Revolution 1788–1802. London: Blackie & Son, 1975.

Index includes references to elections.

562. Knights, M.
Norwich elections for the last 100 years. *Hickling's Almanac*, 1880 p57–99.

563. McKisack, May.
The parliamentary representation of the English boroughs during the Middle Ages. Oxford: O.U.P., 1932 (1962 reprint, London: Frank Cass).

Appendix III reprints a bill for parliamentary expenses for the burgesses from Norwich, 1445–6.

564. Swift, David E.
J.J. Gurney and Norwich politics. *Friends Hist. Soc. J.,* XLIX, 1960 p47–58.

Concerns Quakers in election contests, 1818–33.

THETFORD

See **2–3,6, 20–1, 26, 30, 35, 39–40, 539, 541, 543–4.**

565. Blomefield, Francis.
A history of the ancient city and borough of Thetford. Fersfield, 1739.

Includes a list of MPs, 1546–1735 p182–3.

566. H.O.P.T.
    1509–1558 I, p153–4
    1558–1603 I, p213–4
    1660–1690 I, p332–5
    1715–1754 I, p291–2
    1754–1790 I, p342–3
    1790–1820 II, p295–6

567. Hunt, A. Leigh.
The capital of the ancient kingdom of East Anglia ... being a complete an authentic history of the ancient borough town of Thetford and its antiquities in Norfolk and Suffolk. London: A.G. Dennant, 1870.

Appendix 13 lists parliamentary representatives from 1546 to 1870, with some very brief notes.

NORTHAMPTONSHIRE

See **2, 6, 19–21, 26, 30, 35, 38–9.**

568. BRIDGES, JOHN.
The history and antiquities of Northamptonshire; compiled from the manuscript collections of the late learned antiquary John Bridges by the Rev. Peter Whalley. 2 vols. Oxford: D. Prince, 1791.

> List of MPs for the county (1290 to 1722) Vol 1 p9–11; for Brackley (1547–1720) Vol 1 p144; for Higham Ferrers (1558–1714) Vol 2 p170; for Northampton (1295–1714) Vol 1 p434–6; for Peterborough (1547–1714) Vol 2 p539–40.

569. FORRESTER, ERIC GEORGE.
Northamptonshire county elections and electioneering 1695–1832. London: O.U.P., 1941.

> Comprehensive. Includes chronological list of Members.

570. GRUENFELDER, JOHN K.
The parliamentary election in Northamptonshire, 1626. *Northamptonshire Past and Present,* 4, 1968/1969 p159–65.

571. H.O.P.T.
1509–1558 I, p154–5
1558–1603 I, p214–5
1660–1690 I, p335–6
1715–1754 I, p292
1754–1790 I, p343
1790–1820 II, p297–8

572. SWANSON, R. N.
The second Northamptonshire election of 1701. *Northamptonshire Past and Present*, 6, 1978 p29–31.

BRACKLEY

See **2–3, 6, 20, 26, 30, 35, 39–40, 568.**

573. BAKER, GEORGE.
The history and antiquities of the county of Northampton. 2 vols. London: John Bowyer Nichols, 1822–41.

> Vol 1. Section on Borough representation of Brackley p569–71, including a list of MPs, 1547–1826, with notes. Incomplete.

574. H.O.P.T.
1509–1558 I, p155–7
1558–1603 I, p215–6
1660–1690 I, p336–7
1715–1754 I, p292
1754–1790 I, p343–4
1790–1820 II, p298–9

HIGHAM FERRERS

See **2–3, 6, 20, 26, 30, 35, 39–40, 568.**

575. GROOME, A. N.
Higham Ferrers elections in 1640; a Midland market town on the eve of the Civil War. *Northamptonshire Past And Present,* II (5), 1958 p243–51.

576. H.O.P.T.
1509–1558 I, p157
1558–1603 I, p216
1660–1690 I, p337–8
1715–1754 I, p293
1754–1790 I, p344
1790–1820 II, p299–300

577. V.C.H. NORTHAMPTONSHIRE
Vol III, 1930 p271.

NORTHAMPTON

See **2–3, 6, 20–1, 26, 30, 32, 35, 38–40, 568.**

578. HATLEY, VICTOR A.
The Northampton election of 1774: an eye-witness account. Kettering: Northamptonshire Antiquarian Society, 1968. (Reprinted from the Society's Reports & Papers, 1958 & 1959). (Northampton Historical Series, No.5).

579. H.O.P.T.
1509–1558 I, p157–8
1558–1603 I, p216–7
1660–1690 I, p338–41
1715–1754 I, p293–4
1754–1790 I, p344–7
1790–1820 II, p300–2

580. RECORDS OF THE BOROUGH OF NORTHAMPTON. 2 Vols. Northampton: Birdsall & Son, 1948. (Vol 1; edited by Christopher A. Markham. Vol 2; edited by J. Charles Cox).

Vol 2: Section 13, discusses Members of Parliament. Covers 1328–1831.

581. V.C.H. NORTHAMPTONSHIRE
Vol III, 1930 p17–19.

PETERBOROUGH

See **2, 6, 10, 20–1, 26, 30, 35, 39–40, 568.**

582. H.O.P.T.
    1509–1558 I, p158–60
    1558–1603 I, p217–9
    1660–1690 I, p341–3
    1715–1754 I, p294
    1754–1790 I, p347–8
    1790–1820 II, p302–3

583. V.C.H. NORTHAMPTONSHIRE
    Vol II, 1906 p429.

NORTHUMBERLAND

See **1–2, 6, 17–18, 20–1, 26, 30, 35, 38–9.**

584. BLAIR, CHARLES HENRY HUNTER.
Members of Parliament for Northumberland and Newcastle upon Tyne. *Archaeologia Aeliana,* 4th Series X, 1933 p140–177 (1258–Jan 1327); XI, 1934 p21–82 (Sep 1327–Sep 1399); XII, 1935 p82–132 (Oct 1399–Jan 1558); XIII, 1936 p59–94 (1295–1377); XXIII, 1946 p102–55 (1559–1831).

585. HALCROW, ELIZABETH M.
The election campaigns of Sir Charles Miles Lambert Monck. *Archaeologia Aeliana*, 4th Ser. XXXVI, 1958 p101–22.

Refers to 1812 and 1818 county elections.

586. A HISTORICAL and descriptive view of the county of Northumberland and of the town and county of Newcastle-upon-Tyne with Berwick on Tweed . . . 2 vols. Newcastle-upon-Tyne: Mackenzie & Dent, 1811.

The appendix in Vol 2 lists MPs for Newcastle, 1298–1795, with brief annotations, for Northumberland, 1298–1808 and for Morpeth, 1553–1807.

587. H.O.P.T.
    1509–1558 I, p160–1
    1558–1603 I, p219
    1660–1690 I, p343–4
    1715–1754 I, p294–6
    1754–1790 I, p348
    1790–1820 II, p303–7

588. KILKENNY, C. D.
The Northumberland election, 1826, by C.D. Kilkenny and L. Turnbull. University of Newcastle-upon-Tyne Department of Education, 1970. (Archive Teaching Units No.6).

A "Jackdaw": includes facsimile documents. Refers only to the county.

589. NORTHUMBERLAND COUNTY HISTORY COMMITTEE.
A history of Northumberland. 15 vols. Newcastle-upon-Tyne: Andrew Reid, Sons & Co., 1893–1940.

> Does not cover the whole of the county. Parliamentary representation mentioned briefly for Bamborough and Corbridge.

590. WATTS, SHELDON J.
From border to middle shire: Northumberland 1589–1625. Leicester: L.U.P., 1975.

> Scattered references to Members of Parliament for the county.

BAMBOROUGH

See **589.**

BERWICK-ON-TWEED

See **1–3, 6, 17, 20–1, 26, 29–30, 35, 39–40, 594.**

591. BLAIR, CHARLES HENRY HUNTER.
Members of Parliament for Berwick-upon-Tweed and Morpeth (1558–1831). *Archaeologia Aeliana*, XXIV, 1947 p71–112.

592. H.O.P.T.
    1509–1558 I, p161–2
    1558–1603 I, p219–20
    1660–1690 I, p344–6
    1715–1754 I, p296–7
    1754–1790 I, p348–9
    1790–1820 II, p307–10

CORBRIDGE

See **589.**

MORPETH

See **1–3, 6, 10, 17, 20–1, 26, 30, 35, 39–40, 586, 591, 594.**

593. H.O.P.T.
    1509–1558 I, p162–3
    1558–1603 I, p220–1
    1660–1690 I, p346–7
    1715–1754 I, p297–8
    1754–1790 I, p349–50
    1790–1820 II, p310–1

NEWCASTLE-ON-TYNE

See **1–3, 6–7, 17, 20–1, 23, 26, 30, 35, 38–40, 584, 586.**

594. BLAIR, CHARLES HENRY HUNTER.
Members of Parliament for Newcastle on Tyne, 1377–1588; Berwick, 1529–1558; Morpeth, 1553–1558. *Archaeologia Aeliana* 4th Ser. XIV, 1937 p22–66.

595. H.O.P.T.
   1509–1558 I, p163–4
   1558–1603 I, p221–2
   1660–1690 I, p347–9
   1715–1754 I, p298
   1754–1790 I, p350–1
   1790–1820 II, p311–2

596. HOWELL, ROGER, *Junior.*
Newcastle-upon-Tyne and the Puritan revolution: a study of the Civil War in North England. Oxford: Clarendon Press, 1967.

   Ch.5: The political life of Newcastle 1645–62, concentrates mainly on municipal politics but also covers parliamentary elections.

597. MACKENZIE, ENEAS.
A descriptive and historical account of the town and county of Newcastle-upon-Tyne, including the borough of Gateshead. 2 Vols. Newcastle-upon-Tyne: Mackenzie & Dent, 1827.

   Brief section on MPs in Vol 2, with a list, 1298–1826.

598. MIDDLEBROOK, SYDNEY.
Newcastle-upon-Tyne: its growth and achievement. 2nd ed. Wakefield: S.R. Publishers, 1968.

   Scattered references in the index. Ch.XV: Distress, discontent and political agitation, describes the pressure for reform of the franchise in the early 19th century.

NOTTINGHAMSHIRE

See **2–3, 6, 19–21, 26, 30, 34–5, 38–9.**

599. GOLBY, JOHN.
The great electioneer and his motives: the fourth Duke of Newcastle. *Hist. J.*, 8, 1965, p201–18.

   Discusses his influence in Nottinghamshire, Newark, East Retford, Boroughbridge and Aldborough.

600. H.O.P.T.
   1509–1558 I, p164–6
   1558–1603 I, p222–3
   1660–1690 I, p349–51
   1715–1754 I, p298–9
   1754–1790 I, p351
   1790–1820 II, p312–3

601. OWEN, L. V. D.
The representation of Nottingham and Nottinghamshire in the early parliaments. *Thoroton Soc. Trans.*, XLVII, 1943 p20–8.

   Covers the city and the county only.

602. SEDDON, P. R.
The Nottinghamshire elections for the Short Parliament of 1640. *Thoroton Soc. Trans.*, 80, 1976 p63−8.

Refers to the county and its boroughs.

603. V.C.H. NOTTINGHAMSHIRE
Vol I, 1906 p317−64.

Very brief. Mentions the boroughs.

604. WOOD, ALFRED CECIL.
A history of Nottinghamshire. Nottingham: Thoroton Society, 1947.

Includes references to the electoral history of the county, and of East Retford, Newark, and Nottingham.

605. WOOD, ALFRED CECIL.
Nottinghamshire in the Civil War. Oxford: Clarendon Press, 1937.

Appendix 1 lists Nottinghamshire, Nottingham and East Retford MPs 1640−60. Other references to political history.

EAST RETFORD

See **2−3, 6, 14, 20−1, 26, 29−30, 35, 39−40, 599, 602−5.**

606. H.O.P.T.
1558−1603 I, p223−4
1660−1690 I, p351−2
1715−1754 I, p299−300
1754−1790 I, p352−3
1790−1820 II, p313−5

607. PIERCY, JOHN S.
The history of Retford in the county of Nottingham ... Retford: the author, 1828.

Ch.IV discusses representative history. Covers contested elections 1571−1802, the election of 1826, and lists MPs from 1315 to 1826.

608. PRESTON, R. A.
East Retford: the last days of a Rotten Borough. *Thoroton Soc. Trans.*, 78, 1974 p94−103.

609. SEDDON, P. R.
A parliamentary election at East Retford, 1624. *Thoroton Soc. Trans.*, 76 1972 p26−34.

NEWARK-ON-TRENT

See **2−3, 6, 12, 19, 21, 26, 30, 35, 39−40, 599, 602−4.**

610. BROWN, CORNELIUS.

The annals of Newark-upon-Trent, comprising the history, curiosities and antiquities of the Borough. London: Sotheran & Co., 1879.

Brief discussion, which includes a list of representatives from 1661 to 1874.

611. H.O.P.T.

1660–1690 I, p352–5
1715–1754 I, p300–1
1754–1790 I, p353–5
1790–1820 II, p316–7

612. SMITH, M. J.

Politics in Newark in the 1790s. *Thoroton Soc. Trans.* 84, 1981 p59–67.

NOTTINGHAM

See 2–3, 6–8, 20–1, 23, 26, 29–30, 35, 38–40, 601–5.

613. H.O.P.T.

1509–1558 I, p166–8
1558–1603 I, p224–5
1660–1690 I, p355–6
1715–1754 I, p301–2
1754–1790 I, p355
1790–1820 II, p317–20

614. ORANGE, JAMES.

History and antiquities of Nottingham ... 2 Vols. London: Hamilton, Adams & Co., 1840.

Vol 1, Ch.10 covers political and parliamentary history.

615. THOMIS, M. I.

Politics and society in Nottingham 1785–1835. Oxford: Basil Blackwell, 1969.

Ch.8: The parliamentary borough, p143–68.

OXFORDSHIRE

See 2–3, 6, 20–1, 26, 30, 35, 38–9.

616. DANNATT, G.H.

The Oxfordshire election of 1754: an archive teaching-unit prepared by a joint working party set up by the Oxfordshire County Record Office and the Oxfordshire Education Committee; compiled by G.H. Dannatt. Oxford: Oxfordshire County Council, 1970.

Reproduces contemporary documents.

617. DAVENPORT, JOHN MARRIOTT.

Oxfordshire: Lords Lieutenant, High Sheriffs and Members of Parliament etc; compiled in 1868 by the late John Marriott Davenport; revised by Thomas Marriott Davenport. Oxford: Clarendon Press, 1888.

Includes names of those elected 1290–1886, with biographical footnotes.

OXFORDSHIRE

618. H.O.P.T.
    1509–1558 I, p168–9
    1558–1603 I, p226
    1660–1690 I, p356–7
    1715–1754 I, p302
    1754–1790 I, p356
    1790–1820 II, p320–1

619. ROBSON, R. J.
The Oxfordshire election of 1754: a study in the interplay of city, county and university politics. Oxford: O.U.P., 1949.

Includes references to Oxford City and Oxford University.

620. V.C.H. OXFORDSHIRE
Vol I, 1939 p429–56.

More detail is given post-Civil War, mainly on the city and county. All boroughs mentioned.

621. WILLIAMS, WILLIAM RETLAW.
The parliamentary history of the County of Oxford, including the City and University of Oxford, and the boroughs of Banbury, Burford, Chipping Norton, Dadington, Witney and Woodstock ... 1213–1899. Brecknock: Edwin Davies, 1899.

Arranged in chronological order of elections, based on the Official Return. Includes biographies of the Members.

BANBURY

See **2–3, 6, 20–1, 26, 30, 35, 39–40, 620–1.**

622. BEESLEY, ALFRED.
The history of Banbury. London: Nichols & Son, 1841.

Brief biographical details are given throughout the work. A list of those mentioned is given in the index.

623. H.O.P.T.
    1509–1558 I, p169–70
    1558–1603 I, p226–7
    1660–1690 I, p357–8
    1715–1754 I, p302–3
    1754–1790 I, p356
    1790–1820 II, p321–3

624. JOHNSON, WILLIAM PONSONBY.
History of Banbury and its neighbourhood. Banbury: G. Walford, 1860.

Some discussion of elections and local representatives scattered throughout the text. No index.

625. POTTS, WILLIAM.

A history of Banbury: the story of the development of a country town. Banbury: The Banbury Guardian, 1958.

Ch.XXXII: The pocket borough, p201−7.

626. V.C.H. OXFORDSHIRE

Vol X, 1972 p89−95.

BURFORD

See **620−1.**

627. MONK, W. J.

History of Burford. London: Simpkin, Marshall, Hamilton, Kent & Co., 1891.

Parliamentary representation mentioned p13.

CHIPPING NORTON

See **620−1.**

DADINGTON

See **620−1.**

628. V.C.H. OXFORDSHIRE

Vol XI, 1983 p83−4.

OXFORD

See **2−3, 6, 16, 20−1, 26, 30, 35, 38−40, 619−21.**

629. CANNON, JOHN.

The parliamentary representation of the City of Oxford 1754−90. *Oxoniensia*, XXV, 1960 p102−8.

630. FASNACHT, RUTH.

History of the city of Oxford. Oxford: Basil Blackwell, 1954.

Ch.XIII: The unreformed corporation, includes details of parliamentary elections.

631. H.O.P.T.

1509−1558 I, p171−2
1558−1603 I, p228−9
1660−1690 I, p359−60
1715−1754 I, p305
1754−1790 I, p357−9
1790−1820 II, p325−7

632. V.C.H. OXFORDSHIRE

Vol IV, 1979 p63−4 (1268−1452); p150−4 (1660−1770); p248−54 (1771−1966).

OXFORD UNIVERSITY

See **2–3, 6, 20–1, 26, 30, 35, 39–40, 619–21, 984–5.**

633. GASH, NORMAN.
Peel and the Oxford University election of 1829. *Oxoniensia*, IV, 1939 p162–73.

634. H.O.P.T.
1660–1690 I, p360–2
1715–1754 I, p305–7
1754–1790 I, p359–60
1790–1820 II, p327–31

WITNEY

See **620–1.**

635. MONK, W. J.
History of Witney. Witney: J. Knight, 1894.

Section on parliamentary representatives, p24–6.

WOODSTOCK

See **2, 6, 20–1, 26, 30, 35, 39–40, 620–1.**

636. BALLARD, ADOLPHUS.
Chronicles of the Royal Borough of Woodstock: compiled from the borough records and other original documents. Oxford: Alden & Co., 1896.

Brief references to parliamentary elections.

637. H.O.P.T.
1509–1558 I, p170–1
1558–1603 I, p227–8
1660–1690 I, p358–9
1715–1754 I, p303–5
1754–1790 I, p357
1790–1820 II, p323–5

638. WING, WILLIAM.
Parliamentary history of the borough of Woodstock during the present century. Oxford; 1873. (Reprinted from the Oxford Chronicle?)

Elections 1802–1832 mentioned briefly. Mainly deals with post-1832 history.

RUTLAND

See **2–3, 6, 20–1, 24, 26, 30, 35, 38–9, 531.**

639. H.O.P.T.
    1509–1558 I, p172
    1558–1603 I, p229
    1660–1690 I, p362
    1715–1754 I, p307–8
    1754–1790 I, p360
    1790–1820 II, p331–2

640. V.C.H. RUTLAND
    Vol I, 1908 p165–209.

> Brief references, best found via the index.

SHROPSHIRE

See **2–3, 6, 20–1, 23, 26, 30, 35, 38–9.**

641. H.O.P.T.
    1509–1558 I, p173–4
    1558–1603 I, p229–30
    1660–1690 I, p362–3
    1715–1754 I, p308–9
    1754–1790 I, p360–1
    1790–1820 II, p332

642. HULBERT, CHARLES.
The history and description of the county of Salop ... Vol II, in connection with the enlarged edition of Phillips' History of Shrewsbury. Shrewsbury: the author, 1837.

> Appendix lists Knights of the Shire, 1660–1835. See also Phillips' History **(661)**.

643. JENKINS, A. P.
Two Shropshire elections of the late 18th and early 19th centuries. *Caradoc and Severn Valley Field Club Trans.*, 16, Nov 1968 p124–8.

644. V.C.H. SHROPSHIRE
    Vol III, 1979 p232–358.

> Very good account. Divided into periods, then into separate sections for each borough. Includes maps showing constituency boundaries in 1832 and 1918.

645. WEYMAN, HENRY T.
Shropshire Members of Parliament. *Shropshire Arch. Soc. Trans.*, 4th series (X), 1925–6 pl–32 and 161–92; (XI), 1927–8 pl–48 and 153–84; (XII), 1929–30 pl–47 and pxvi.

> Chronological list of Members elected 1290–1880, with substantial biographies.

BISHOP'S CASTLE

See **2–3, 6, 20, 23, 26, 29–30, 35, 39–40, 644.**

646. Burton, J. R.
Two elections for Bishop's Castle in the 18th century. *Shropshire Arch. Soc. Trans.*, (Ser.3), IX p266.

Refers to 1741 and 1753.

647. H.O.P.T.
1558–1603 I, p230–1
1660–1690 I, p363–4
1715–1754 I, p309–10
1754–1790 I, p361–2
1790–1820 II, p332–4

648. Weyman, Henry T.
The Members of Parliament for Bishop's Castle. *Shropshire Arch. Soc. Trans.*, 2nd series (10), 1898 p33–68.

BRIDGNORTH

See 2–3, 6, 20–1, 23, 26, 30, 35, 38–40, 644.

649. H.O.P.T.
1509–1558 I, p174–5
1558–1603 I, p231
1660–1690 I, p364–5
1715–1754 I, p310–1
1754–1790 I, p362–3
1790–1820 II, p335–6

650. Mason, J. F. A.
The borough of Bridgnorth 1157–1957. Bridgnorth: Bridgnorth Borough Council, 1957.

Ch.5: The Whitmores and Bridgnorth, p28–34. Covers 1660–1870.

651. Weyman, Henry T.
The Members of Parliament for Bridgnorth. *Shropshire Arch. Soc. Trans.*, 4th Series (V), 1915 pl–76.

The same format as Weyman's *Shropshire Members of Parliament* (645).

LUDLOW

See 2–3, 6, 20, 23, 26, 30, 35, 38–40, 644.

652. H.O.P.T.
1509–1558 I, p175–7
1558–1603 I, p231–2
1660–1690 I, p365–6
1715–1754 I, p311
1754–1790 I, p363
1790–1820 II, p336

653. WEYMAN, HENRY T.
The Members of Parliament for Ludlow. *Shropshire Arch. Soc. Trans.*, 2nd Series (VII), 1895 pl−54; 4th Series (III), 1913 piii-iv.

MUCH WENLOCK

See **2, 6, 20−1, 23, 26, 30, 35, 38−40, 644.**

654. FORREST, H. E.
The old houses of Wenlock and Wenlock Edge: their history and associations. 2nd ed. Shrewsbury: Wilding & Son, 1915.

Appendix E lists MPs from 1472 to 1880.

655. H.O.P.T.
1509−1558 I, p177−8
1558−1603 I, p232−3
1660−1690 I, p366−7
1715−1754 I, p312
1754−1790 I, p364
1790−1820 II, p339−41

656. WEYMAN, HENRY T.
The Members of Parliament for Wenlock. *Shropshire Arch. Soc. Trans.*, 3rd Series (II), 1902 p297−358.

Covers 1472−1880.

SHREWSBURY

See **2, 6, 10, 20−1, 23, 26, 30, 35, 38−40, 644.**

657. EDWARDS, EDWARD.
Parliamentary elections of the Borough of Shrewsbury, from 1283 to 1859. Shrewsbury: Edward Edwards, 1859.

Originally published in the Shrewsbury Chronicle. Detailed accounts of each election with biographical material, arranged in chronological order. Some factual details of election dates etc. inaccurate, perhaps because it was published before the Official Return. No index.

658. GRUENFELDER, JOHN K.
The parliamentary election for Shrewsbury, 1604. *Shropshire Arch. Soc. Trans.*, 59, 1973/1974 p272−7.

659. H.O.P.T.
1509−1558 I, p178−80
1558−1603 I, p233−4
1660−1690 I, p367−8
1715−1754 I, p311−2
1754−1790 I, p363−4
1790−1820 II, p336−9

SHROPSHIRE

660. HOUGHTON, K.N.
A document concerning the parliamentary election at Shrewsbury in 1478. *Shropshire Arch. Soc. Trans.*, 57, 1961/4 p162−5.

661. PHILLIPS, THOMAS.
The history and antiquities of Shrewsbury, from its first foundation to the present time. 2nd ed. 2 Vols. Shrewsbury: the author, 1837.

Vol 1, Ch.IX: Parliamentary elections 1709−1830.

662. WEYMAN, HENRY T.
Shrewsbury Members of Parliament. *Shrophire Arch. Soc. Trans.*, 4th Series (XII), 1929−30 p113−272; (XLVII), 1933−4 pi-ii.

Contains a chronological list of Members elected 1295−1918, with extensive biographies of each.

SOMERSET

See 2−3, 6, 20−1, 26, 30, 35, 38−9, 187.

663. BARNES, THOMAS GARDEN.
Somerset 1625−1640: a county's government during the "personal rule". London: O.U.P., 1961.

References throughout the work. Covers mainly the county, but also Bath, Bridgwater, Ilchester, Milborne Port, Minehead, Taunton and Wells.

664. FARNHAM, EDITH.
Somerset election of 1614. *E.H.R.*, 46, October 1931 p579−99.

665. HARBIN, SOPHIA WYNDHAM BATES.
Members of Parliament for the County of Somerset. Taunton: Somersetshire Archaeological and Natural History Society, 1939.

Biographies of Members from 1258 to 1832 in chronological order, with an index.

666. H.O.P.T.
1509−1558 I, p180
1558−1603 I, p234
1660−1690 I, p368−70
1715−1754 I, p312−3
1754−1790 I, p365
1790−1820 II, p341−3

667. PHELPS, W.
The history and antiquities of Somersetshire. 2 Vols. London: J.B. Nichols & Son, 1839.

Vol, Ch.VII Parliamentary history, includes list of Knights of the Shire, 1298−1835.

668. UNDERDOWN, DAVID.
Somerset in the Civil War and interregnum. Newton Abbot: David & Charles, 1973.

> Focusses on the county, but also mentions Bath, Milborne Port, Bridgwater, Minehead, Taunton, Ilchester and Wells. References scattered.

669. V.C.H. SOMERSET
Vol II, 1911 p173−243.

> Better discussion of post 1640 than the early period. Mentions all boroughs.

AXBRIDGE

See **669.**

BATH

See **2−3, 6, 20−1, 26, 30, 35, 38−40, 663, 668−9.**

670. H.O.P.T.
1509−1558 I, p180−1
1558−1603 I, p234−5
1660−1690 I, p370−3
1715−1754 I, p313−4
1754−1790 I, p366−7
1790−1820 II, p343−4

BRIDGWATER

See **2−3, 6, 20−1, 26, 29−30, 35, 38−40, 663, 668−9.**

671. H.O.P.T.
1509−1558 I, p181−2
1558−1603 I, p235
1660−1690 I, p372−4
1715−1754 I, p314
1754−1790 I, p367−8
1790−1820 II, p345−6

672. JARMAN, SYDNEY GARDNOR.
A history of Bridgwater. London: Elliot Stock, 1889.

> Ch.XXV: The political history, p149−59.

673. POWELL, ARTHUR HERBERT.
Bridgwater in the later days. Bridgwater: Page & Son, 1908.

> Covers 18th and 19th centuries. Ch.XIX includes a list of MPs from 1702−1868.

CHARD

See **669.**

DUNSTER

See **669.**

674. LYTE, *Sir* H. C. Maxwell.
A history of Dunster and of the families of Mohun and Luttrell. 2 Vols.
London: St Catherine Press, 1909.

> Mentions Dunster briefly. Discusses elections in Minehead, but references are scattered.

ILCHESTER

See **2–3, 6, 10, 20, 22, 26, 29–30, 35, 39–40, 198, 663, 668–9.**

675. COX, J. STEVENS.
A history of Ilchester, the ancient county town of Somerset. Ilchester: J. Stevens Cox, 1958.

> Notes on Ilchester political history, p218–25. Includes list of Members, 1298–1832.

676. H.O.P.T.
1660–1690 I, p374–5
1715–1754 I, p314–5
1754–1790 I, p368
1790–1820 II, p346–50

677. UNDERDOWN, DAVID.
The Ilchester election, February 1646. *Somersetshire Arch. Soc. Trans.*, 110, 1966 p40–51.

678. V.C.H. SOMERSET
Vol III, 1974 p194–6.

LANGPORT

See **669.**

679. ROSS, DAVID MELVILLE.
Langport and its church: the story of the ancient borough, with references to neighbouring parishes. Langport: Herald Press, 1911.

> Brief note of the election of Langport MPs, p162–3.

MILBORNE PORT

See **2–3, 6, 8, 10, 20, 26, 30–1, 35, 39–40, 663, 668–9.**

680. H.O.P.T.
1660–1690 I, p375–6
1715–1754 I, p315–6
1754–1790 I, p368–9
1790–1820 II, p350–2

MINEHEAD

See **2–3, 6, 20, 26, 29–30, 35, 39–40, 663, 668–9, 674.**

681. HANCOCK, F.
Minehead in the county of Somerset: a history of the parish, the manor and the port. Taunton: Barnicott & Pearce, 1903.

Ch.5: Political history, includes a list of MPs, 1562–1833.

682. H.O.P.T.
1558–1603 I, p235–6
1660–1690 I, p376–7
1715–1754 I, p316–7
1754–1790 I, p369–71
1790–1820 II, p352–3

MONTAGUE

See **669.**

STOKE CURSI

See **669.**

TAUNTON

See **2–3, 6, 10, 20–1, 26, 29–30, 35, 38–40, 663, 668–9.**

683. H.O.P.T.
1509–1558 I, p182–4
1558–1603 I, p236–7
1660–1690 I, p378–9
1715–1754 I, p317–8
1754–1790 I, p371–2
1790–1820 II, p353–5

684. TOULMIN, JOSHUA.
The history of Taunton, in the county of Somerset. New ed., by James Savage. Taunton: John Poole, 1822.

Ch.III, Civil constitution of the town, includes its parliamentary representation, with accounts of the general elections between 1714 and 1820 as regards Taunton, and a list of MPs from 1409 to 1820.

WATCHET

See **669.**

685. WEDLAKE, A. LESLIE.
A history of Watchet. Watchet: the author, 1955.

Parliamentary representation mentioned briefly.

WELLS

See 2–3, 6, 20–1, 26, 35, 38–40, 663, 668–9.

686. H.O.P.T.
    1509–1558 I, p184–5
    1558–1603 I, p237
    1660–1690 I, p379–81
    1715–1754 I, p318
    1754–1790 I, p373–4
    1790–1820 II, p355–7

WERE

See **669.**

STAFFORDSHIRE

See 2–3, 6, 20–1, 26, 30, 35, 38–9.

687. Burne, Sambrooke A.H.
The Staffordshire county election, 1747. Stafford: the author, 1967.

688. Greene, Donald J.
The politics of Samuel Johnson. Port Washington, New York: Kennikat Press, 1960 (1973 reprint).

> Chapter 2(2): The politics of Staffordshire, p34–44. Concerns Lichfield and Newcastle-under-Lyme as well as the county.

689. Hackwood, Frederick William.
Glimpses of bygone Staffordshire. Lichfield: Mercury Press, 1925. (Reprinted from the Lichfield Mercury).

> Ch.XIV: Parliamentary representatives of Staffordshire. Mentions the boroughs as well as the county.

690. Hardy, S.M.
The downfall of the Gower interest in the Staffordshire boroughs, 1800–30, by S.M. Hardy and R.C. Bailey. *Collections for a History of Staffordshire for 1950–1,* 1954 p265–301.

691. H.O.P.T.
    1509–1558 I, p185–6
    1558–1603 I, p238–41
    1660–1690 I, p381–3
    1715–1754 I, p318–9
    1754–1790 I, p374
    1790–1820 II, p357–8

692. Staffordshire County Council. *Education Department*
Staffordshire elections 1715–1832. Staffordshire County Council, 1969. (Local History Source Books No.5).

> An interesting collection of reprinted source materials. Covers the boroughs as well as the county.

693. V.C.H. STAFFORDSHIRE
Vol I, 1908 p217–73.

> Not covered in detail, but all boroughs mentioned.

694. WEDGWOOD, JOSIAH CLEMENT.
Staffordshire parliamentary history from the earliest times to the present day. 3 volumes in 4 parts. William Salt Archaeological Society, 1919–1933. Vol I (1213–1603), London: Harrison & Sons, 1919. Vol II, Part I (1603–1715), London: Harrison & Sons, 1920. Vol II, Part II (1715–1832), London: Harrison & Sons, 1922. Vol III (1780–1841), Kendal: Titus Wilson & Son, 1934.

> Arranged in chronological order of date of elections, with biographical information. Includes tables of the Staffordshire peerage and a 1747 map of the county. Vol II Part II only covers elections for the period 1715–1780, although it discusses prominent political families up to 1832 in its introduction. Each volume is indexed.

695. WORDIE, JAMES R.
Estate management in eigthteenth century England: the building of the Leveson-Gower fortune. London: Royal Historical Society, 1982.

> Ch.5: The political dimension, discusses the influence of the family in the county and in Lichfield, Newcastle, Stafford and Tamworth.

LICHFIELD

See **2–3, 6–7, 20–1, 26, 30, 35, 39–40, 688–90, 692–5.**

696. HARWOOD, THOMAS.
The history and antiquities of the church and city of Lichfield. Gloucester: Joseph Harris, 1806.

> Brief discussion of representative history p361–7, which includes a list of Members from 1553–1802.

697. H.O.P.T.
1509–1558 I, p186–7
1558–1603 I, p241–2
1660–1690 I, p383–7
1715–1754 I, p319–20
1754–1790 I, p374–5
1790–1820 II, p358–60

698. JOSTEN, C.H.
Elias Ashmole and the 1685 Lichfield election. *Collections for a History of Staffordshire for 1950–1.*, 1954, p215–27.

699. PARKER, ALFRED, D.
A sentimental journey in and about the ancient and loyal city of Lichfield. Lichfield: A.C. Lomax's successors, 1925.

> Ch.13: Politics and elections. Also lists MPs 1799–1924, p148–9.

700. WILLIAMS, ALFRED.
Sketches in and around Lichfield and Rugeley. Lichfield: Eggington & Brown, 1892.

Parliamentary representation mentioned briefly, p243–4.

NEWCASTLE-UNDER-LYME

See **2–3, 6, 14, 16, 20–1, 26, 29–30, 35, 38–40, 688–90, 692–5.**

701. H.O.P.T.
1509–1558 I, p187–8
1558–1603 I, p242–3
1660–1690 I, p387–8
1715–1754 I, p320
1754–1790 I, p375
1790–1820 II, p360–2

702. PAPE, THOMAS.
Medieval Newcastle-under-Lyme. Manchester: M.U.P., 1928. (Publications of the University of Manchester No. CLXXXVII).

Ch.XI: The parliamentary representation of Newcastle-under-Lyme. Includes a list of MPs, 1354–1509.

703. PAPE, THOMAS.
Newcastle-under-Lyme in Tudor and early Stuart times. Manchester: M.U.P., 1938. (Publications of the University of Manchester No. CCLXI).

Ch.V: The parliamentary representation of Newcastle-under-Lyme from 1509 to 1603. Includes a list of MPs.

704. V.C.H. STAFFORDSHIRE
Vol VIII, 1963 p42–4.

STAFFORD

See **2–3, 6, 14, 20–1, 26, 30, 35, 38–40, 689–90, 692–5.**

705. H.O.P.T.
1509–1558 I, p188–9
1558–1603 I, p243–4
1660–1690 I, p388–9
1715–1754 I, p320–1
1754–1790 I, p375
1790–1820 II, p362–4

706. V.C.H. STAFFORDSHIRE
Vol VI, 1979 p237–8.

TAMWORTH

See **2–3, 6, 20–1, 26, 30, 35, 39–40, 689–90, 692–5.**

707. H.O.P.T.
  1558–1603 I, p244–5
  1660–1690 I, p390–2
  1715–1754 I, p321–2
  1754–1790 I, p376–7
  1790–1820 II, p365

708. PALMER, CHARLES FERRERS.
The history of the town and castle of Tamworth, in the counties of Stafford & Warwick. Tamworth: Jonathan Thompson, 1845.

> Many references in the index. List of MPs in the appendix, pxi-xiv, covering 1563–1841.

709. STUART, D.G.
'Castle' and 'manor': parliamentary patronage in the borough of Tamworth in the mid-18th century. *Lichfield Arch. and Hist. Soc. Trans.*, IX, 1968 p59–65.

710. WOOD, HENRY.
Borough by prescription: a history of the municipality of Tamworth. Tamworth: Tamworth Corporation, 1958.

> Ch.IV: Municipal and parliamentary elections. Covers 1563–1949. No list of MPs.

711. WOOD, HENRY.
Tamworth borough records: being a catalogue of civic records with appendices. Tamworth: Johnson & Allsopp, 1952.

> Section VII: Parliamentary elections, describes records covering 1669–1872, with notes.

SUFFOLK
See 2–3, 6, 19–21, 26, 30, 35, 38–9, 534, 726.

712. FITCH, W.S.
Election expenses of Sir John Howard and Thomas Brewse: election for Knights of the Shire, 20 April 1467. *Suffolk Arch. Assn. Original Papers* Pt 2 June 1847 p4–6. Further note. *Proc. of the Suffolk Institute of Archaeology* 2, 1854–9, p206–7.

713. H.O.P.T.
  1509–1558 I, p189–90
  1558–1603 I, p245–6
  1660–1690 I, p392–4
  1715–1754 I, p322
  1754–1790 I, p377
  1790–1820 II, p366–7

714. PAGE, AUGUSTINE.
A topographical and genealogical history of the county of Suffolk. Ipswich: Frederick Pawsey, 1847.

> Appendix lists Members for Ipswich, Suffolk and Bury St Edmunds, 1768–1844.

715. SUCKLING, ALFRED.
The history and antiquities of the county of Suffolk. 2 Vols. London: John Weale, 1846–8. Index, Ipswich: W.S. Cowell, 1952.

Lists Knights of the Shire, 1542–1837, and MPs for Dunwich 1298–1832.

716. V.C.H. SUFFOLK
Vol II, 1907 p157–98.

Parliamentary representation discussed at the end. All boroughs mentioned briefly.

717. VIRGOE, ROGER.
Three Suffolk parliamentary elections of the mid-fifteenth century. *B.I.H.R.*, 39, Nov 1966 p185–96.

Elections in 1453, 1455, and 1472.

ALDEBURGH

See **2–3, 6, 20, 26, 30, 35, 39–40, 716.**

718. CLODD, H.P.
Aldeburgh: the history of an ancient borough. Ipswich: Norman Adlard & Co., 1959.

Ch.11: Elections, covers 1566–1832.

719. HELE, NICHOLAS FENWICK.
Notes or jottings about Aldeburgh, Suffolk, relating to matters historical, antiquarian, ornithological and entomological. 2nd ed., Ipswich: S. & W.J. King, 1890.

List of Members from 1571–1831, p64–6.

720. H.O.P.T.
1558–1603 I, p246–7
1660–1690 I, p394–6
1715–1754 I, p322–3
1754–1790 I, p378
1790–1820 II, p367–9

BURY ST EDMUNDS

See **2–3, 6, 20–1, 26, 30, 35, 39–40, 714, 716.**

721. H.O.P.T.
1660–1690 I, p396–8
1715–1754 I, p323–4
1754–1790 I, p378–9
1790–1820 II, p369

722. MURRELL, PAT E.
Bury St Edmunds and the campaign to pack Parliament 1687–8. *B.I.H.R.*, LIV, November 1981 p188–206.

DUNWICH

See 2−3, 6, 20, 26, 30, 35−6, 38−40, 715−6.

723. H.O.P.T.
    1509−1558 I, p190−1
    1558−1603 I, p247
    1660−1690 I, p398−400
    1715−1754 I, p324
    1754−1790 I, p379
    1790−1820 II, p369−70

EYE

See 2−3, 6, 20−1, 26, 30, 35, 39−40, 716.

724. H.O.P.T.
    1558−1603 I, p247−8
    1660−1690 I, p400−2
    1715−1754 I, p324−5
    1754−1790 I, p379−80
    1790−1820 II, p370−1

IPSWICH

See 2−3, 6, 19−22, 26, 30, 35, 38−40, 714, 716.

725. H.O.P.T.
    1509−1558 I, p191−2
    1558−1603 I, p248−9
    1660−1690 I, p402−4
    1715−1754 I, p325
    1754−1790 I, p380−1
    1790−1820 II, p371−4

726. REDSTONE, LILIAN J.
Ipswich through the ages. Ispwich: East Anglian Magazine, 1948.

    Brief references to Ipswich and Suffolk elections.

727. SANSOM, J.
Payments to Members of Parliament for Ipswich, 1448−1680. *Notes and Queries* 2nd Series. 4, 1859 p273.

ORFORD

See 2−3, 6, 20, 23, 26, 30, 35, 39−40, 716.

728. H.O.P.T.
    1509−1558 I, p192−3
    1558−1603 I, p249−50
    1660−1690 I, p404−5
    1715−1754 I, p325−6
    1754−1790 I, p381−2
    1790−1820 II, p374

SUDBURY

See 2–3, 6, 10, 20–1, 26, 29–31, 35, 39–40, 716.

729. GRIMWOOD, C.G.
History of Sudbury, Suffolk, by C.G. Grimwood and S.A. Kay.
Sudbury: the authors, 1953.

    Ch.XI: Parliamentary representation, p108–12.

730. GURDON, W.B.
A Sudbury election in 1699. *East Anglian* N.S.5, 1893/4 p33–5.
(Gurdon Papers No. 6).

731. H.O.P.T.
    1558–1603 I, p250
    1660–1690 I, p405–7
    1715–1754 I, p327
    1754–1790 I, p382–3
    1790–1820 II, p374–7

SURREY

See 2–3, 6, 20–1, 26, 30, 35, 38–9.

732. BRAYLEY, EDWARD WEDLAKE.
A topographical history of Surrey. 5 Vols. Dorking: Robert Best Ede,
1841–48.

    Vol I: Notes on the county, with a list of the Knights of the Shire, 1796–1841.
    Also notes on Guildford. Vol III: Kingston. Vol IV: Reigate, with a list of
    MPs, 1796–1841; Bletchingley, with a list of MPs, 1796–1832; Gatton, with a
    list of MPs, 1796–1832. Vol V: Farnham; Haslemere, with a list of MPs,
    1796–1832; Southwark, with a list of MPs, 1796–1847. Each volume
    separately indexed.

733. H.O.P.T.
    1509–1558 I, p193
    1558–1603 I, p250–1
    1660–1690 I, p407–8
    1715–1754 I, p327–8
    1754–1790 I, p383–4
    1790–1820 II, p377–9

734. MALDEN, H.E.
Notes on parliamentary representation in Surrey. *Surrey Arch. Collections*, 39, 1930, p51–64.

    Covers the county and its boroughs.

735. MANNING, OWEN.
The history and antiquities of the county of Surrey ...; by Rev. Owen
Manning and William Bray. 3 Vols. London: John White, 1804–1814.

    Includes information relating to the county, Guildford, Reigate, Haslemere,
    Gatton, Bletchingley and Southwark.

736. SMITH, JOHN EDWARD.
Parliamentary representation of Surrey from 1290 to 1924 ... London: Wightman & Co., 1927.

> Discusses both county and boroughs. Includes separate lists of Members returned for each.

737. TURNER, J.S.T.
An Augustan election: the 1710 general election in the county of Surrey. *Surrey Arch. Collections*, 68, 1971 p131–51.

> Mentions all boroughs except Farnham and Kingston.

738. V.C.H. SURREY
Vol I, 1902 p329–444.

> Overall treatment brief, but mentions all boroughs. Lists Knights of the Shire, 1290–1880.

BLETCHINGLEY

See 2–3, 6, 14, 20, 26, 30, 35, 38–40, 732, 734–8.

739. H.O.P.T.
1509–1558 I, p193–4
1558–1603 I, p251–2
1660–1690 I, p408–9
1715–1754 I, p328–9
1754–1790 I, p384–5
1790–1820 II, p379–80

740. LAMBERT, UVEDALE.
Bletchingley: a short history. Guildford: Surrey Archaeological Society, 1949.

> Interesting mention of early 19th century political control, p34–6.

741. LAMBERT, UVEDALE.
Bletchingley: a parish history together with some account of the family of De Clare chiefly in the south of England. 2 Vols. London: Mitchell Hughes & Clarke, 1921.

> Vol 1, Appendix gives Knights of the Shire for Surrey (1290–1832) and Members for Bletchingley (1295–1832).

742. V.C.H. SURREY
Volume IV, 1912 p255–6.

FARNHAM

See 732, 734, 736, 738.

743. V.C.H. SURREY
Vol II, 1905 p590.

SURREY

GATTON

See **2–3, 6, 20, 26, 30, 35, 38–40, 732, 734–8.**

744. H.O.P.T.
    1509–1558 I, p194–5
    1558–1603 I, p252–3
    1660–1690 I, p409–10
    1715–1754 I, p329
    1754–1790 I, p385
    1790–1820 II, p380–1

745. V.C.H. SURREY
    Vol III, 1911 p196–7.

GUILDFORD

See **2–3, 6, 20–1, 26, 30, 35, 38–40, 732, 734–8.**

746. H.O.P.T.
    1509–1558 I, p195–6
    1558–1603 I, p253
    1660–1690 I, p410–1
    1715–1754 I, p329
    1754–1790 I, p385–6
    1790–1820 II, p381–2

747. RUSSELL, J.
The history of Guildford, the county town of Surrey. Guildford: J. & S. Russell, 1801.

Guildford a Borough-town, p170–3. Brief. Covers 1678–1738.

748. V.C.H. SURREY
    Voll III, 1911 p562.

HASLEMERE

See **2–3, 6, 10, 20, 26, 30, 35, 39–40, 732, 734–8.**

749. H.O.P.T.
    1558–1603 I, p253–4
    1660–1690 I, p411–3
    1715–1754 I, p329–30
    1754–1790 I, p386–7
    1790–1820 II, p382–3

750. ROLSTON, G.R.
Haslemere in history. Haslemere: G.R. Rolston, 1957.

Parliamentary representation, p61–4.

751. SWANTON, E.W.
  Bygone Haslemere: a short history of the ancient borough and its immediate neighbourhood from earliest times; edited by E.W. Swanton aided by P. Woods. London: West, Newman & Co, 1914.

  Ch.XVI: Early political history;
  Ch.XVII: General Oglethorpe and the elections;
  Ch.XVIII: Later political history.
  Appendix D: Procedure at a parliamentary election, 1759.

752. V.C.H. SURREY
  Vol III, 1911 p47.

KINGSTON-ON-THAMES
See **732, 734, 736, 738.**

753. V.C.H. SURREY
  Vol III, 1911 p499.

REIGATE
See **2−3, 6, 20−1, 26, 30, 35, 38−40, 732, 734−8.**

754. H.O.P.T.
  1509−1558 I, p196−7
  1558−1603 I, p254
  1660−1690 I, p413−4
  1715−1754 I, p330
  1754−1790 I, p387
  1790−1820 II, p383−4

755. HOOPER, WILFRED.
  Reigate: its story through the ages. Guildford: Surrey Archaeological Society, 1945.

  Ch.VIII: Parliamentary history. Covers 1295 to 1867.

756. PHILLIPS, ROBERT.
  A geological, historical and topographical description of the borough of Reigate and surrounding district; edited by T.R. Hooper. Redhill: the author, 1885.

  Parliamentary history, p43−4. Rather short.

757. V.C.H. SURREY
  Vol III, 1911 p234.

SOUTHWARK
See **2−3, 6, 13−14, 20−1, 26, 29−30, 35, 38−40, 732, 734−8.**

758. CLIFFORD, HENRY.
  A report of the two cases of controverted elections of the Borough of Southwark in the County of Surrey ... London: W. Clarke & Sons, 1802.

  Refers to 1796−7. Covers Southwark and Canterbury.

759. H.O.P.T.
    1509–1558 I, p197–9
    1558–1603 I, p254–5
    1660–1690 I, p414–7
    1715–1754 I, p330–1
    1754–1790 I, p387–8
    1790–1820 II, p384–7

760. V.C.H. SURREY
    Vol IV, 1912 p139.

SUSSEX

See **2–3, 6, 20–1, 26, 30, 35, 38–9.**

761. BARTTELOT, *Sir* WALTER B.
Extract from the Return of Members of Parliament 1290–1702. *Sussex Arch. Soc. Collections*, 30, 1880 p190–7.

> Entries from the name index for eight Sussex families: Ashburnham, Barttelot, Courthope, Gage, Goring, Pelham, Shelley and West. Not very useful.

762. BEDDARD, R. A.
The Sussex general election of 1695: a contemporary account by Robert Middleton, Vicar of Cuckfield. *Sussex Arch. Soc. Collections*, 106, 1968 p145–57.

> Refers to the county and Chichester.

763. COOPER, WILLIAM DURRANT.
The parliamentary history of the county of Sussex and of the several boroughs and Cinque Ports therein. Lewes: Baxter, 1834.

> Covers Arundel, Bramber, Brighton (post 1832), Chichester, East Grinstead, Horsham, Lewes, Midhurst, New Shoreham, Steyning and the Sussex Cinque Ports: Hastings, Rye, Seaford and Winchelsea. Reprinted as an Appendix to Horsfield (**767**).

764. FLETCHER, ANTHONY.
A county community in peace and war: Sussex 1600–1660. London: Longmans, 1975.

> Part IV: Politics. Covers the county and the boroughs.

765. HESS, ROBERT L.
The Sackville family and Sussex politics: the campaign for the by-election, 1741. *Sussex Arch. Soc. Collections*, 99, 1961 p20–37.

766. H.O.P.T.
    1509–1558 I, p199–200
    1558–1603 I, p255
    1660–1690 I, p417–8
    1715–1754 I, p331–2
    1754–1790 I, p388
    1790–1820 II, p387–90

767. HORSFIELD, THOMAS WALKER.
History, antiquities and topography of the county of Sussex. 2 Vols,
Lewes: Sussex Press, 1835.

> Appendix, p23–75: Parliamentary history, by W.D. Cooper. A reprint of **763**.

768. McCANN, T. J.
Crocket and the Sussex county by-election of 1741. *Sussex Arch. Soc.
Collections* 114, 1976 p121–5.

769. McQUISTON, JULIAN R.
Sussex aristocrats and the county election of 1820. *E.H.R.*, 88, July 1973
p534–58.

770. NADEL, G. H.
The Sussex election of 1741. *Sussex Arch. Soc. Collections*, 91, 1953
p84–124.

771. POLL for the election of members of Parliament for the county of Sussex,
1705. *Sussex Record Soc. Publications,* 4, 1905 p22–67.

> Copy of a poll referred to in Cooper **(763)**.

772. STENNING, ALAN H.
A return (so far as they can be ascertained) of the Members of Parliament
for the county and boroughs of Sussex. *Sussex Arch. Soc. Collections,*
30, 1880 p161–89 (1290–1368). Ibid., 31, 1881 p95–122 (1369–1421).
Ibid., 32, 1882 p140–66 (1422–1558). Ibid., 33, 1883 p69–100
(1558–1681). Ibid., 35, 1887 p127–64 (1685–1754).

> Transcribed in chronological order of Parliament, just as in the O.R. Not very
> useful.

773. SWALES, R. J. W.
The Howard interest in Sussex elections 1529–1558. *Sussex Arch. Soc.
Collections*, 114, 1976 p49–60.

> Mainly concerned with Bramber, Horsham, Lewes and Shoreham as well as the
> county.

774. V.C.H. SUSSEX
Vol I, 1905 p481–539.

> Treatment brief, though some detail on 18th century. Mentions all boroughs.

775. WILLIAMS, BASIL.
The Duke of Newcastle and the election of 1734. *E.H.R.*, XII, 1897
p448–88.

> Covers also Lewes, Seaford and Shoreham.

ARUNDEL

See 2–3, 6, 14, 20–1, 26, 30, 35, 37–40, 763–4, 772, 774.

776. EUSTACE, G. W.
    Arundel: borough and castle. London: Robert Scott, 1922.

    Mentioned in passing throughout the book.

777. H.O.P.T.
    1509–1558 I, p200–1
    1558–1603 I, p255–6
    1660–1690 I, p418
    1715–1754 I, p332–3
    1754–1790 I, p388–9
    1790–1820 II, p390–1

BRAMBER

See **2–3, 6, 20, 26, 30, 35, 38–40, 763–4, 772–4.**

778. H.O.P.T.
    1509–1558 I, p210–2
    1558–1603 I, p256–7
    1660–1690 I, p418–20
    1715–1754 I, p333
    1754–1790 I, p390
    1790–1820 II, p391–2

791. V.C.H. SUSSEX
    Vol VI Part 1, 1980 p211–2.

    Opening sentences identical to Steyning.

CHICHESTER

See **2–3, 6, 20–1, 24, 26, 30, 35, 38–40, 762–4, 772, 774.**

780 HAY, ALEXANDER.
    The history of Chichester. Chichester: J. Seagrave, 1804.

    Includes list of MPs, 1660–1804.

781. H.O.P.T.
    1509–1558 I, p202–3
    1558–1603 I, p257–8
    1660–1690 I, p420–1
    1715–1754 I, p333–4
    1754–1790 I, p390–2
    1790–1820 II, p392–3

782. V.C.H. SUSSEX
    Vol III, 1935 p98–100.

EAST GRINSTEAD

See **2–3, 6, 20, 26, 29–30, 35, 38–40, 763–4, 772, 774.**

783. HILLS, WALLACE HENRY.
The history of East Grinstead. East Grinstead: Farncombe & Co., 1906.

> Ch.III: The borough of East Grinstead and its Members of Parliament. Includes list with biographical notes, 1301–1831. Further information goes up to 1906.

784. H.O.P.T.
1509–1558 I, p203–4
1558–1603 I, p258–9
1660–1690 I, p421–3
1715–1754 I, p334–5
1754–1790 I, p392–3
1790–1820 II, p393–4

HASTINGS

See **962–6.**

HORSHAM

See **2–3, 6, 12, 20–1, 26, 30, 35, 38–40, 763–4, 772–4.**

785. ALBERY, WILLIAM.
A parliamentary history of the ancient borough of Horsham, 1295–1885. London: Longmans, Green & Co., 1927.

> Includes a chronological and an alphabetical list of Members returned. Contains many illustrations, including portraits of Members.

786. COPLEY, JOHN S.
Report of the proceedings before the Select Committee of the House of Commons, appointed the 8th of January 1807, in the case of a double return for the borough of Horsham, in the county of Sussex. London: J. Butterworth, 1808.

> Mainly contains technical arguments about the franchise.

787. H.O.P.T.
1509–1558 I, p204–5
1558–1603 I, p259
1660–1690 I, p423–4
1715–1754 I, p335
1754–1790 I, p393
1790–1820 II, p394–5

788. WINDRUM, ANTHONY.
Horsham: an historical survey. London: Phillimore, 1978.

> Ch.2: Parliamentary and local government p44–60. Interesting and easy to read. Lacks references.

LEWES

See **2–3, 6, 20–1, 26, 30, 32, 35, 38–40, 763–4, 772–5.**

789. ELECTION expenses, Lewes, 1727. *Sussex Notes and Queries,* 2, 1928–9, p58–60.

790. HILLS, WALLACE HENRY.
The parliamentary history of the borough of Lewes, 1295–1885. Reprinted, with additions from the East Sussex News. Lewes: Farncombe & Co., 1908.

Adds to earlier studies and includes information not in the Official Return. Arranged in chronological order of election, with biographical and other details.

791. H.O.P.T.
1509–1558 I, p205–6
1558–1603 I, p259–60
1660–1690 I, p424
1715–1754 I, p335–6
1754–1790 I, p393–5
1790–1820 II, p395–7

792. HORSFIELD, THOMAS WALKER.
The history and antiquities of Lewes and its vicinity ... 2 vols. Lewes: J. Baxter, 1824–7.

Appendix IV, Vol I lists MPs from 1298–1820, with notes.

793. V.C.H. SUSSEX
Vol VII, 1940 p31.

MIDHURST

See **2–3, 6, 20–1, 26, 29–30, 35, 38–40, 763–4, 772, 774.**

794. CRAWFURD, G. P.
Midhurst in parliament, 1660–1832. *Sussex County Mag.* XXI (12), 1947 p382–4.

795. H.O.P.T.
1509–1558 I, p206–7
1558–1603 I, p260–1
1660–1690 I, p424–5
1715–1754 I, p336
1754–1790 I, p395–6
1790–1820 II, p397–8

796. V.C.H. SUSSEX
Vol IV, 1953 p76.

RYE

See **971–3.**

SEAFORD

See **976–8.**

SHOREHAM

See **2–3, 6, 20–1, 26, 30, 35, 37–40, 763–4, 772–5.**

797. CHEAL, HENRY.
The story of Shoreham. Hove: Combridges, 1921.

> Ch.XIV: Parliamentary history, includes a list of MPs from 1295 to 1885, with biographical notes.

798. FRY, GEORGE S.
Robert Frye, MP for Shoreham, 1385, 1391, 1396–7 and 1399. *Sussex Notes and Queries*, 4, 1932 p62–3.

799. H.O.P.T.
> 1509–1558 I, p207–8
> 1558–1603 I, p261
> 1660–1690 I, p425–6
> 1715–1754 I, p337–8
> 1754–1790 I, p396–9
> 1790–1820 II, p398–9

STEYNING

See **2, 6, 12, 20, 26, 30, 35, 38–40, 763–4, 772, 774.**

800. H.O.P.T.
> 1509–1558 I, p208–9
> 1558–1603 I, p262
> 1660–1690 I, p427
> 1715–1754 I, p338
> 1754–1790 I, p399
> 1790–1820 II, p399

801. SCHAFER, R. G.
A by-election in a rotten borough. *Huntingdon Library Q.*, XVII, 1954 p397–405.

> Refers to 1726.

802. V.C.H. SUSSEX
Vol VI Part 1, 1980 p240–1.

> Opening sentences identical to Bramber.

WINCHELSEA

See **979–81.**

WARWICKSHIRE

See **2–3, 6–7, 20–1, 26, 30, 35, 38–9.**

803. H.O.P.T.
  1509−1558 I, p209−10
  1558−1603 I, p262−3
  1660−1690 I, p427−9
  1715−1754 I, p339
  1754−1790 I, p399−400
  1790−1820 II, p400−1

804. V.C.H. WARWICKSHIRE
  Vol II, 1908 p421−68.

   Treatment brief; includes boroughs.

COVENTRY
See **2−3, 6−7, 20−1, 23, 26, 29−30, 35, 38−40, 804.**

805. HARRIS, MARY DORMER.
Memoirs of Rt Hon Edward Hopkins, MP for Coventry. *E.H.R.*
XXXIV, 1919, p491−504.

   Describes the election at Coventry in 1701.

806. H.O.P.T.
  1509−1558 I, p211−2
  1558−1603 I, p263
  1660−1690 I, p429−31
  1715−1754 I, p339−41
  1754−1790 I, p400−2
  1790−1820 II, p401−4

807. SMITH, FREDERICK.
Coventry: six hundred years of municipal life. Coventry: Coventry City
Corporation, 1946.

   Includes references to parliamentary representation.

808. V.C.H. WARWICKSHIRE
  Vol III, 1969 p248−55.

809. WHITLEY, THOMAS WALKER.
The parliamentary representation of the city of Coventry from the earliest
times to the present date. Coventry: Curtis & Beamish, 1894.

   Apart from the lack of an index, a good example of an interesting and valuable
   constituency history. Well illustrated. MPs 1295−1892 listed in Appendix 1.

WARWICK
See **2−3, 6, 16, 20−1, 26, 30, 35, 38−40, 804.**

810. H.O.P.T.
  1509−1558 I, p212−4
  1558−1603 I, p263−4
  1660−1690 I, p431−3
  1715−1754 I, p341
  1754−1790 I, p402−3
  1790−1820 II, p404−5

811. KEMP, THOMAS.
The black book of Warwick; transcribed and edited by Thomas Kemp. Warwick: Henry T. Cooke & Son, 1898.

Index includes references to some interesting documents on elections.

812. KEMP, THOMAS.
A history of Warwick and its people. Warwick: Henry T. Cooke & Son, 1905.

Several references to parliamentary elections in the index.

813. KEMP, THOMAS.
A list of Members of Parliament for Warwick, and for Warwick and Leamington from 1885, by T. Kemp and A.B. Beaven. Warwick: Henry H. Lacy, 1912.

Covers 1213–1910. Compiled from the Official Return. Some biographical notes.

814. V.C.H. WARWICKSHIRE
Vol VIII, 1969 p476–504.

WESTMORLAND

See **1–3, 6, 17–21, 26, 30, 35, 38–9, 165–6.**

815. DOUGLAS, W. W.
Wordsworth in politics: the Westmorland election of 1818. *Modern Language Notes*, 63, November 1948 p437–49.

816. FERGUSON, RICHARD SAUL.
A history of Westmorland. London: Elliot Stock, 1894.

Brief references to the parliamentary representation of Westmorland and Appleby.

817. GREEN, DAVID BONNELL.
Wordsworth in the Westmorland election of 1818: a new letter to John Taylor. *Modern Language R.,*62, Oct 1967 p606–7.

818. H.O.P.T.
1509–1558 I, p214–5
1558–1603 I, p264–5
1660–1690 I, p433–5
1715–1754 I, p341–2
1754–1790 I, p403–4
1790–1820 II, p405–8

819. WASHINGTON, GEORGE S. H. L.
Early Westmorland MPs 1258–1327. Kendal: Titus Wilson, 1959. (Cumberland and Westmorland Antiquarian and Archaeological Society Tract Series No XV).

Includes information not contained in the Official Return. Lists Members returned for Westmorland and Appleby in chronological order of their election, followed by substantial biographies of each in alphabetical order.

APPLEBY

See **1–3, 6, 17, 20, 26, 30, 35–6, 38–40, 165–6, 816, 819.**

820. H.O.P.T.
      1509–1558 I, p215–6
      1558–1603 I, p265–6
      1660–1690 I, p435–6
      1715–1754 I, p342–3
      1754–1790 I, p404–6
      1790–1820 II, p408–10

WILTSHIRE

See **2–3, 6, 20–1, 26, 30, 35, 38–9.**

821. CANNON, JOHN A.
The Wiltshire election of 1772: an interpretation. *Wiltshire Arch. and Natural History Mag.*, LVII, 1960 p386–90.

822. H.O.P.T.
      1509–1558 I, p216–8
      1558–1603 I, p266–9
      1660–1690 I, p436–7
      1715–1754 I, p343
      1754–1790 I, p406–8
      1790–1820 II, p410–3

823. MANLEY, F. H.
A list of the representatives in Parliament from 1295–1832 for the county and boroughs of Wiltshire, as given in the Parliamentary Return of 1872. *Wiltshire Arch. and Natural History Mag.*, XLVII, 1935 p177–264.

Covers the county and all its boroughs, with brief notes.

824. RATHBONE, MAURICE G.
List of Wiltshire borough records earlier in date than 1836; edited by Maurice G. Rathbone. Devizes, Wiltshire Archaeological and Natural History Society, 1951.

There are Chapters on Calne, Chippenham, Devizes, Downton, Heytesbury, Malmesbury, Marlborough, Salisbury, Wilton and Wootton Bassett. Records relating to elections usually given a separate section. No index.

825. ROWE, VIOLET A.
The influence of the Earls of Pembroke on parliamentary elections, 1625–41. *E.H.R.,* L, 1935 p242–56.

Mainly in Wiltshire and Cornwall.

826. STUCKEY, ROBERT G.
An analysis of the parliamentary representation of Wiltshire, 1688–1714. *Wiltshire Arch. and Natural History Mag.*, LIV, 1951–2 p289–304.

Covers the county and its boroughs in general terms.

827. V.C.H. WILTSHIRE
Vol V, 1957 p72−230.

> Very good treatment. Split into periods. All boroughs mentioned.

BRADFORD

See **823, 826−7.**

828. V.C.H. WILTSHIRE
Vol VII, 1953 p38.

CALNE

See **2−3, 6, 20−1, 26, 30, 35, 38−40, 823−4, 826−7.**

829. H.O.P.T.
1509−1558 I, p218−9
1558−1603 I, p269
1660−1690 I, p437−9
1715−1754 I, p343
1754−1790 I, p408
1790−1820 II, p413−4

830. MARSH, A. E. W.
History of the borough and town of Calne. London: Castle, Lambe & Storr, 1903.

> Part I: Calne. Includes a list of MPs, 1295−1885.

CHIPPENHAM

See **2−3, 6, 14, 16, 20−1, 26, 29−30, 35, 38−40, 823−4, 826−7.**

831. DANIELL, J. J.
The history of Chippenham. Chippenham: R.F. Houlston, 1894.

> Section on Members of Parliament, p67−75. Lists them from 1801−1880.

832. GOLDNEY, FREDERICK HASTINGS.
Records of Chippenham: relating to the Borough from ... 1554 to ... 1889. London: Diprose, Bateman & Co., 1889.

> Lists MPs for Chippenham, 1295−1885.

833. H.O.P.T.
1509−1558 I, p219−20
1558−1603 I, p269−70
1660−1690 I, p439−41
1715−1754 I, p343−4
1754−1790 I, p408−9
1790−1820 II, p414−6

CRICKLADE

See **2−3, 6, 10, 20−2, 26, 30, 35, 38−40, 823, 826−7.**

834. CRICKLADE HISTORICAL SOCIETY.
Materials for a history of Cricklade. Cricklade: Cricklade Historical Society, 1949.

> Ch.VI: The parliamentary borough and its Members. In chronological order of Parliaments, with biographical details and notes of election petitions.

835. H.O.P.T.
1509–1558 I, p220–1
1558–1603 I, p270–1
1660–1690 I, p441–2
1715–1754 I, p344–5
1754–1790 I, p409–11
1790–1820 II, p416–8

836. PETRIE, SAMUEL.
Report of the Cricklade case. London: Thomas Payne & Son, 1785.

> A full report of corrupt practices at the election in 1780.

DEVIZES

See **2–3, 6, 20–1, 26, 30, 35, 38–40, 823–4, 826–7.**

837. H.O.P.T.
1509–1558 I, p221–1
1558–1603 I, p271
1660–1690 I, p442–4
1715–1754 I, p345
1754–1790 I, p411–2
1790–1820 II, p418

838. V.C.H. WILTSHIRE
Vol X, 1975 p284–5.

DOWNTON

See **2–3, 6, 10, 20, 22, 26, 30, 35, 38–40, 823–4, 826–7.**

839. H.O.P.T.
1509–1558 I, p222–3
1558–1603 I, p271–2
1660–1690 I, p444–5
1715–1754 I, p345
1754–1790 I, p412–3
1790–1820 II, p419

840. V.C.H. WILTSHIRE
Vol XI, 1980 p45–6.

GREAT BEDWIN

See **2–3, 6, 19–20, 26, 30, 35, 38–40, 823, 826–7.**

841. H.O.P.T.
  1509–1558 I, p223–4
  1558–1603 I, p272–3
  1660–1690 I, p445–7
  1715–1754 I, p346
  1754–1790 I, p413–4
  1790–1820 II, p419–20

842. WARD, J.
  The representative history of Great Bedwyn. *Wiltshire Arch. and Natural History Mag.*, VI, 1860 p291–2.

HEYTESBURY

See **2, 6, 20, 26, 30, 35, 38–40, 823–4, 826–7.**

843. CANNON, JOHN A.
  Borough of Heytesbury in the eighteenth century. *Wiltshire Arch. and Natural History Mag.*, LVII, 1960 p223–4.

844. H.O.P.T.
  1509–1558 I, p224–5
  1558–1603 I, p273
  1660–1690 I, p447–8
  1715–1754 I, p346–7
  1754–1790 I, p414–5
  1790–1820 II, p420–1

HINDON

See **2–3, 6, 10, 20, 26, 30, 35, 38–40, 823, 826–7.**

845. H.O.P.T.
  1509–1558 I, p225
  1558–1603 I, p273–4
  1660–1690 I, p449–50
  1715–1754 I, p347
  1754–1790 I, p415–6
  1790–1820 II, p421

846. V.C.H. WILTSHIRE
  Vol XI, 1980 p101.

LUDGERSHALL

See **2–3, 6, 20, 26, 30, 35, 38–40, 823, 826–7.**

847. H.O.P.T.
  1509–1558 I, p226
  1558–1603 I, p274
  1660–1690 I, p450–1
  1715–1754 I, p347–8
  1754–1790 I, p416–7
  1790–1820 II, p421–2

WILTSHIRE

MALMESBURY

See 2−3, 6, 14, 20−1, 26, 29−30, 35, 38−40, 823−4, 826−7.

848. BOUVERIE, E. O. PLEYDELL.
Malmesbury election petition, 1807. *Wiltshire Arch. and Natural History Mag.*, 36, 1909−10 p292−9.

Refers to an election in October 1806.

849. BROWNE, A. L.
Lord Halifax and the Malmesbury election in 1701. *Wiltshire Arch. and Natural History Mag.*, 47, 1936 p500−3.

850. H.O.P.T.
1509−1558 I, p226−7
1558−1603 I, p274−5
1660−1690 I, p452−3
1715−1754 I, p348−9
1754−1790 I, p417−8
1790−1820 II, p422−4

851. MOFFATT, J. M.
The history of the town of Malmesbury and of its ancient abbey ...
Tetbury: J.G. Goodwyn, 1805.

Section 6 discusses parliamentary history.

852. OSBORN, J. LEE.
Malmesbury. Bristol: J.W. Arrowsmith, 1919.

Ch.3 discusses parliamentary representation briefly.

MARLBOROUGH

See 2−3, 6, 19−21, 26, 30, 35, 38−40, 823−4, 826−7.

853. H.O.P.T.
1509−1558 I, p227−9
1558−1603 I, p275
1660−1690 I, p453−5
1715−1754 I, p349−50
1754−1790 I, p418−9
1790−1820 II, p424

854. V.C.H. WILTSHRIE
Vol XII, 1983 p219−20.

855. WAYLEN, JAMES.
A history military and municipal of the town (otherwise called the city) of Marlborough. London: John Russell Smith, 1854.

Ch.VII includes accounts of the elections in 1679, 1689 and 1714.

MERE

See **823, 826–7.**

OLD SARUM

See **2, 6, 19–20, 26, 30, 35–6, 38–40, 402, 823, 826–7, 860.**

856 H.O.P.T.
1509–1558 I, p229–30
1558–1603 I, p275–6
1660–1690 I, p455–6
1715–1754 I, p350–1
1754–1790 I, p419
1790–1820 II, p424–6

857. V.C.H. WILTSHIRE
Vol VI, 1962 p66–7.

SALISBURY

See **2–3, 6, 16, 20–1, 26, 30, 35, 38–40, 823–4, 826–7.**

858. DRYDEN, ALICE.
Memorials of old Wiltshire; edited by Alice Dryden. London: Bemrose & Sons, 1906.

> Chapter on Salisbury politics in the reign of Queen Anne (p107–15) describes an election in 1705 in Salisbury.

859. H.O.P.T.
1509–1558 I, p230–1
1558–1603 I, p276
1660–1690 I, p456–7
1715–1754 I, p351
1754–1790 I, p419–20
1790–1820 II, p426–7

860. HOARES, *Sir* RICHARD COLT.
The history of modern Wiltshire: Old and New Sarum, or Salisbury, by Robert Benson and Henry Hatcher. London: John Bowyer Nichols & Son, 1843.

> Contains very little information on parliamentary representation, apart from lists of Members for Old and New Sarum.

861. V.C.H. WILTSHIRE
Vol VI, 1962 p103–5, 117–24.

WESTBURY

See **2, 6, 20–1, 26, 30, 35, 38–40, 823, 826–7.**

862. CUNNINGTON, B. H.
A parliamentary election at Westbury in 1747. *Wiltshire Arch. and Natural History Mag.*, XLIX, 1938 p540.

WILTSHIRE

863. H.O.P.T.
    1509−1558 I, p231−2
    1558−1603 I, p277
    1660−1690 I, p457−9
    1715−1754 I, p351−2
    1754−1790 I, p420
    1790−1820 II, p427−8

864. V.C.H. WILTSHIRE
    Vol VIII, 1965 p185.

WILTON

See **2−3, 6, 20−1, 26, 30, 35, 38−40, 823−4, 826−7.**

865. H.O.P.T.
    1509−1558 I, p232−3
    1558−1603 I, p277
    1660−1690 I, p459−60
    1715−1754 I, p352−3
    1754−1790 I, p420−1
    1790−1820 II, p428−9

866. V.C.H. WILTSHIRE
    Vol VI, 1962 p27−8.

WOOTTON BASSETT

See **2−3, 6, 20, 26, 30, 35, 38−40, 823−4, 826−7.**

867. DICKINSON, H. T.
Henry St. John, Wootton Bassett, and the general election of 1708. *Wiltshire Arch. and Natural History Mag.*, 64, 1969 p107−11.

868. GINGELL, P. J.
The history of Wootton Bassett: "a very ancient mayor towne". Wootton Bassett: Wootton Bassett Historical Society, 1977.

    Ch.V: The political arena, is relevant. Appendix 3 lists MPs, 1446−1832.

869. H.O.P.T.
    1509−1558 I, p233−4
    1558−1603 I, p277−8
    1660−1690 I, p460−1
    1715−1754 I, p353
    1754−1790 I, p421−2
    1790−1820 II, p429−30

870. V.C.H. WILTSHIRE
    Vol IX, 1970 p198.

WORCESTERSHIRE

See **2, 6, 20−1, 26, 30, 35, 38−9.**

871. GROSVENOR, IAN D.
Catholics and politics: the Worcestershire election of 1604. *Recusant History*, 14, May 1978 p149–62.

872. H.O.P.T.
1509–1558 I, p234–5
1558–1603 I, p278–9
1660–1690 I, p461–2
1715–1754 I, p353–4
1754–1790 I, p422
1790–1820 II, p430–1

873. V.C.H. WORCESTERSHIRE
Vol II, 1906 p197–234.

Quite good. All boroughs mentioned, but separate paragraphs for Bewdley, Droitwich, Evesham and Worcester.

874. WILLIAMS, WILLIAM RETLAW.
The parliamentary history of the County of Worcester ... 1213–1897. Hereford: Jakeman & Carver, 1897.

Includes the city of Worcester, and the boroughs of Bewdley, Droitwich, Dudley, Evesham, Kidderminster, Bromsgrove and Pershore. Arranged in chronological order of dates of elections and includes biographical notes.

BEWDLEY

See 2–3, 6, 20–1, 26, 30, 35, 39–40, 873–4.

875. BURTON, JOHN R.
A history of Bewdley; with concise accounts of some neighbouring parishes. London: William Reeves, 1883.

Members from 1614 to 1880 are listed in the appendix, pxxxix-xl. Briefly mentioned in the text.

876. H.O.P.T.
1660–1690 I, p462–4
1715–1754 I, p354–5
1754–1790 I, p422–3
1790–1820 II, p431–2

877. STYLES, P.
The Corporation of Bewdley under the later Stuarts. *University of Birmingham Hist. J.*, 1, 1947 p92–133.

Includes a list of Members.

878. V.C.H. WORCESTERSHIRE
Vol IV, 1924 p302.

BROMSGROVE

See 873–4.

879. LEADBETTER, WILLIAM G.
The story of Bromsgrove. Bromsgrove: Messenger Co., 1946.

Parliamentary representation mentioned, p8.

880. V.C.H. WORCESTERSHIRE
Vol III, 1913 p20.

DROITWICH

See **2−3, 6, 20−1, 26, 30, 35−6, 39−40, 873−4.**

881. H.O.P.T.
1509−1558 I, p235−6
1558−1603 I, p279
1660−1690 I, p464−5
1715−1754 I, p355
1754−1790 I, p423−4
1790−1820 II, p432

882. V.C.H. WORCESTERSHIRE
Vol III, 1913 p78.

DUDLEY

See **21, 30, 873−4.**

883. V.C.H. WORCESTERSHIRE
Vol III, 1913 p99.

EVESHAM

See **2−3, 6, 8, 20−1, 26, 29−30, 35, 39−40, 873−4.**

884. H.O.P.T.
1660−1690 I, p465−7
1715−1754 I, p355
1754−1790 I, p424−5
1790−1820 II, p432−4

885. MAY, GEORGE.
A descriptive history of the town of Evesham. Evesham: George May, 1845.

Ch.XIV: Elective and parliamentary history. Covers 1295−1841, with notes on individual elections from 1604.

886. V.C.H. WORCESTERSHIRE
Vol II, 1906 p372.

KIDDERMINSTER

See **21, 30, 873−4.**

887. V.C.H. WORCESTERSHIRE
Vol III, 1913 p162−3.

PERSHORE

See **873−4.**

888. V.C.H. WORCESTERSHIRE
Vol IV, 1924 p153.

WORCESTER

See **2−3, 6−8, 10, 20−1, 26, 30, 35, 38−40, 873−4.**

889. CHAMBERS, JOHN.
A general history of Worcester. Worcester: William Walcott, 1819.

Brief section on parliamentary history, p386−7.

890. H.O.P.T.
1509−1558 I, p236−8
1558−1603 I, p279−80
1660−1690 I, p467−8
1715−1754 I, p356
1754−1790 I, p425−7
1790−1820 II, p434−5

891. V.C.H. WORCESTERSHIRE
Vol IV, 1924 p389.

YORKSHIRE

See **1−2, 6, 18−21, 26, 30, 35−6, 38−9.**

892. ADDY, JOHN,
Parliamentary elections and reform 1807−1832. London: Longmans, 1961. (Then and there series).

Written for schoolchildren and illustrated from contemporary sources. Discusses the Yorkshire election of 1807 and 1826, and the Pontefract election of 1812.

893. CARTWRIGHT, JAMES J.
Chapters in the history of Yorkshire. Wakefield: B.W. Allen, 1872.

Chapter IV: Yorkshire representatives and their contemporaries, 1603−1628. Includes many contemporary letters.

894. COLLYER, C.
The Yorkshire election of 1734. *Proc. Leeds Philosophical Soc.*, VII, 1952−5 p53−82.

895. COLLYER, C.
The Yorkshire election of 1741. *Proc. Leeds Philosphical Soc.*, VII, 1952−5 p137−52.

896. FLETCHER, J. S.
The making of modern Yorkshire 1750–1914. London: George Allen & Unwin, 1918.

> Ch.VII: Reform, discusses parliamentary representation. Mentions the county in 1807, and the main boroughs: Aldborough, Beverley, Boroughbridge, Hedon, Kingston-on-Hull, Knaresborough, Malton, Northallerton, Pontefract, Richmond, Ripon, Scarborough, Thirsk and York.

897. GASH, NORMAN.
Brougham and the Yorkshire election of 1830. *Proc. Leeds Philosophical Soc.*, VIII, 1956–9 p19–35.

898. GOODER, A.
The parliamentary representation of the County of York, 1258–1832; edited by A. Gooder. 2 Vols. Yorkshire Archaeological Society, 1935.

> Substantial biographical entries as well as useful background in Part I. Covers County Members only.

899. GRUENFELDER, JOHN K.
Yorkshire borough elections, 1603–1640. *Yorkshire Arch. J.*, 49, 1977 p101–14.

> Covers Aldborough, Beverley, Boroughbridge, Hedon, Kingston-on-Hull, Knaresborough, Pontefract, Richmond, Ripon, Scarborough, Thirsk and York.

900. H.O.P.T.
> 1509–1558 I, p238–40
> 1558–1603 I, p280–4
> 1660–1690 I, p468–9
> 1715–1754 I, p357
> 1754–1790 I, p427–32
> 1790–1820 II, p435–40

901. LAWSON-TANCRED, *Sir* THOMAS.
Records of a Yorkshire Manor. London: Edward Arnold, 1937.

> Part II deals with parliamentary history, p197–384, and includes contemporary correspondence. Primary focus is on Aldborough and Boroughbridge, with a list of MPs for both (interfiled) from 1553 to 1831.

902. MARKHAM, JOHN.
Nineteenth century parliamentary elections in East Yorkshire. Beverley: East Yorkshire Local History Society, 1982.

> Covers Hedon, Beverley and Hull; also the East Riding (post 1832), from 1800 to 1872.

903. PARK, GODFREY RICHARD.
Parliamentary representation of Yorkshire ...; compiled by Godfrey Richard Park. Hull: Charles Henry Barnwell, 1886.

Covers the period 1290–1886. Includes sections on the cities of York and Ripon; the Boroughs of Kingston-on-Hull, Knaresborough, Malton, Northallerton, Pontefract, Richmond, Scarborough and Thirsk; the disfranchised Boroughs of Aldborough, Boroughbridge, Beverley and Hedon; and the disused Boroughs of Doncaster, Tickhill, Pickering, Yarm and Ravenser. Contains mainly lists of Members returned in each case. Also covers the constituencies enfranchised after 1832.

904. SALT, S. P.
Sir Thomas Wentworth and the parliamentary representation of Yorkshire, 1614–1628. *Northern History,* 16, 1980 p130–68.

Refers to Yorkshire and Pontefract.

905. SMITH, E. ANTHONY.
The Yorkshire elections of 1806 and 1807: a study in electoral management. *Northern History,* 2, 1967 p62–90.

Covers the county only.

906. SMITH, HENRY STOOKS.
The parliamentary representation of Yorkshire. London: John Russell Smith, 1854.

Chronological list of those elected for each borough and the county itself, so far as was then known. Superseded by the Official Return.

907. SMITH, ROBERT WORTHINGTON.
Political organisation and canvassing: Yorkshire elections before the Reform Bill. *American Hist. R.,* LXXIV (ii), 1969 p1538–60.

Discusses the Yorkshire Association and county elections from 1734 to 1832.

908. SMITH, WILLIAM.
Old Yorkshire; edited by William Smith. 5 Vols. London: Longmans, 1881–84.

Contains chapters on Yorkshire constituencies and MPs (Vol 1), Leeds parliamentary representation (Vol 2) and Halifax parliamentary representation (Vol 5).

909. THOMPSON, F. M. L.
Whigs and Liberals in the West Riding 1830–1860. *E.H.R.,* LXXIV, 1959 p214–39.

910. V.C.H. YORKSHIRE (GENERAL)
Vol III, 1913 p393–434.

Coverage very brief. Boroughs mentioned mainly in 12th and 19th centuries.

ALDBOROUGH

See **1–3, 6, 20, 26, 30, 35, 39–40, 599, 896, 901, 903, 906, 908, 910.**

911. CARROLL, ROY.
The by-election at Aldborough, 1673. *Huntington Library Q.*, XXVIII, 1965 p157−78.

912. H.O.P.T.
1509−1558 I, p240−1
1558−1603 I, p284−5
1660−1690 I, p469−72
1715−1754 I, p357
1754−1790 I, p432
1790−1820 II, p440−1

913. LAWSON-TANCRED, *Sir* THOMAS.
Parliamentary history of Aldborough and Boroughbridge. *Yorkshire Arch. J.*, XXVII, 1923−4 p325−62.

Covers 1553−1700.

914. TURNER, T. S.
History of Aldborough and Boroughbridge. London: Arthur Hall, Virtue & Co., 1853.

Appendix lists separately the MPs for Aldborough and Boroughbridge, 1715 to 1831.

915. WALKER, JOHN WILLIAM.
Records relating to a seventeenth century parliamentary election. *Yorkshire Arch. J.*, 34, 1939 p25−34.

Concentrates on Aldborough 1660−91, but also mentions Scarborough 1450−1.

BEVERLEY

See **1−2, 6, 20−1, 26, 30, 35, 39−40, 896, 899, 902−3, 906, 908, 910.**

916. H.O.P.T.
1558−1603 I, p285−6
1660−1690 I, p472−3
1715−1754 I, p357−8
1754−1790 I, p432−3
1790−1820 II, p441−3

917. POULSON, GEORGE.
Beverlac; or the antiquities and history of the town of Beverley, in the county of York ... 2 Vols. Beverley: George Scaum, 1829.

Representative history Vol 1 p387−98. Includes list of representatives 1295−1826.

BOROUGHBRIDGE

See **1−3, 6, 20, 26, 30, 35, 39−40, 599, 896, 899, 901, 903, 906, 908, 910, 913−4.**

918. H.O.P.T.
    1509–1558 I, p241–2
    1558–1603 I, p286
    1660–1690 I, p473–4
    1715–1754 I, p358
    1754–1790 I, p433–4
    1790–1820 II, p443–5

DONCASTER

See **903, 906, 908, 910.**

HEDON

See **1–3, 6, 20, 26, 30, 35, 39–40, 896, 899, 902, 906, 908, 910.**

919. BOYLE, J. R.
The early history of the town and port of Hedon, in the East Riding of the County of York. Hull: A Brown & Sons, 1895.

Parliamentary representation, p39.

920. H.O.P.T.
    1509–1558 I, p242–4
    1558–1603 I, p286–7
    1660–1690 I, p474–5
    1715–1754 I, p358–9
    1754–1790 I, p434
    1790–1820 II, p445–6

921. MARKHAM, JOHN.
The 1820 parliamentary election at Hedon: a study of electioneering in a Yorkshire borough before the passing of the Reform Act. Beverley: John Markham, 1971.

922. PARK, GODFREY RICHARD.
The history of the ancient borough of Hedon. Hull: W.G.B. Page, 1895.

Substantial section on representative history, with names, biographical details and some portraits.

KINGSTON-ON-HULL

See **1–3, 6–7, 20–1, 26, 30, 35, 38–40, 896, 899, 902–3, 906, 908, 910.**

923. GILLETT, EDWARD.
A history of Hull, by Edward Gillett and Kenneth A. MacMahon. Oxford: O.U.P., 1980.

References scattered throughout.

924. H.O.P.T.
      1509–1558 I, p244–6
      1558–1603 I, p287–8
      1660–1690 I, p475–7
      1715–1754 I, p359–60
      1754–1790 I, p434–5
      1790–1820 II, p446–50

925. SHEAHAN, JAMES JOSEPH.
History of the town and port of Kingston-upon-Hull. 2nd ed. Beverley: John Green, 1866.

> Lists parliamentary representatives 1305–1865, with some discussion, p313–33.

926. V.C.H. YORKSHIRE: EAST RIDING
Vol I, 1969 p39–40, 100–2, 102–7, 201–6.

> Separate sections discuss parliamentary representation, divided into periods.

KNARESBOROUGH

See **1–3, 6, 20–1, 26, 29–30, 35, 39–40, 896, 899, 903, 906, 908, 910.**

927. ATKINSON, W. A.
A parliamentary election in Knaresborough in 1628. *Yorkshire Arch. J.*, 34, 1939 p213–21.

928. H.O.P.T.
      1509–1558 I, p246–8
      1558–1603 I, p288–9
      1660–1690 I, p478–9
      1715–1754 I, p360
      1754–1790 I, p435–6
      1790–1820 II, p450–2

929. JENNINGS, BERNARD.
A history of Harrogate and Knaresborough; written by the Harrogate WEA Local History Group, edited by Bernard Jennings. Huddersfield: Advertiser Press, 1970.

> Ch.VI(d): The Restoration and the beginnings of nonconformity, p154–64; and Ch.XIV(c): Political life to 1868, p354–69.

LEEDS

See **1, 21, 30, 903, 910.**

MALTON

See **1–3, 6, 19–21, 26, 30, 35, 39–40, 896, 903, 906, 908, 910.**

930. H.O.P.T.
    1660–1690 I, p479–80
    1715–1754 I, p360–1
    1754–1790 I, p436
    1790–1820 II, p452–4

931. HUDLESTON, NIGEL A.
History of Malton and Norton. Scarborough: G.A. Pindar & Son, 1962.

MPs listed 1295–1640, p62; and 1640–1885, p130–2. No index.

932. SMITH, E. ANTHONY.
Earl Fitzwilliam and Malton: a proprietary borough in the early nineteenth century. *E.H.R.*, 80, 1965 p51–69.

933. V.C.H. YORKSHIRE: NORTH RIDING
Vol I, 1914 p531–2.

NORTHALLERTON

See **1–3, 6, 20–1, 26, 30, 35, 39–40, 896, 903, 906, 908, 910.**

934. H.O.P.T.
    1660–1690 I, p480–1
    1715–1754 I, p361
    1754–1790 I, p436–7
    1790–1820 II, p454

935. INGLEDEW, C. J. DAVISON.
The history and antiquities of Northallerton in the county of York. London: Bell & Daldy, 1858.

Section on the borough (p126–40) discusses the parliamentary representation and includes a list of Members, 1298–1857, with biographical notes.

936. V.C.H. YORKSHIRE: NORTH RIDING
Vol I, 1914 p422–3.

PICKERING

See **903, 906, 908, 910.**

937. V.C.H. YORKSHIRE: NORTH RIDING
Vol II, 1923 p468.

PONTEFRACT

See **1–3, 6, 10, 12, 14, 20–2, 26, 30, 35, 39–40, 892, 896, 899, 903, 906, 908, 910.**

938. Fox, George.
The history of Pontefract in Yorkshire. Pontefract: John Fox, 1827.

> List of representatives 1620–1820, with biographical notes, p61–3.

939. H.O.P.T.
1660–1690 I, p481–3
1715–1754 I, p361–2
1754–1790 I, p437–8
1790–1820 II, p454–7

RAVENSER

See **903, 906, 908, 910.**

RICHMOND

See **1–3, 6, 20–1, 26, 30, 35, 39–40, 896, 899, 903, 906, 908, 910.**

940. Clarkson, C.
The history of Richmond in the county of York ... Richmond: T. Bowman, 1814.

> Brief account of parliamentary history, p137–43.

941. Fieldhouse, Roger T.
A history of Richmond and Swaledale, by R. Fieldhouse and B. Jennings. London: Phillimore, 1978.

> Ch.13: Politics and parliamentary representation. Based on **942.**

942. Fieldhouse, Roger T.
Parliamentary representation in the borough of Richmond. *Yorkshire Arch. J.*, 44, 1972 p207–16.

943. H.O.P.T.
1558–1603 I, p289–90
1660–1690 I, p483–4
1715–1754 I, p362
1754–1790 I, p438–9
1790–1820 II, p457–8

944. V.C.H. Yorkshire: North Riding
Vol I, 1914 p27.

RIPON

See **1–3, 6, 20–1, 26, 30, 35, 39–40, 896, 899, 903, 906, 908, 910.**

945. H.O.P.T.
1509–1558 I, p248–9
1558–1603 I, p290–1
1660–1690 I, p484–5
1715–1754 I, p363
1754–1790 I, p439
1790–1820 II, p458

SCARBOROUGH

See 1–3, 6, 20–1, 26, 30, 35–6, 38–40, 896, 899, 903, 906, 908, 910, 915.

946. BAKER, JOSEPH BROGDEN.
The history of Scarborough from the earliest date. London: Longmans, 1882.

A good municipal history. Section 9: Parliamentary history of the borough. Includes list of MPs from 1253 to 1880, with brief biographical notes.

947. FORSTER, GORDON C. G.
Elections at Scarborough for the Long Parliament, 1640–7. *Scarborough and District Arch. Soc. Trans.*, 1, 1960 p3–9.

948. HINDERWELL, THOMAS.
The history and antiquities of Scarborough. 3rd ed. Scarborough: J. Bye, 1832.

Parliamentary history, p132–45, includes a list of representatives, 1283–1832, with brief biographical notes.

949. H.O.P.T.
1509–1558 I, p249–50
1558–1603 I, p291–2
1660–1690 I, p485–7
1715–1754 I, p363–4
1754–1790 I, p439–41
1790–1820 II, p458–60

950. V.C.H. YORKSHIRE: NORTH RIDING
Vol II, 1923 p551.

THIRSK

See 1–3, 6, 20–1, 26, 30, 35, 39–40, 896, 899, 903, 906, 908, 910.

951. H.O.P.T.
1509–1558 I, p250–1
1558–1603 I, p292
1660–1690 I, p487–9
1715–1754 I, p364
1754–1790 I, p441
1790–1820 II, p460–1

952. V.C.H. YORKSHIRE: NORTH RIDING
Vol II, 1923 p61.

TICKHILL

See 903, 906, 908, 910.

YARM

See 903, 906, 908, 910.

953. V.C.H. YORKSHIRE. NORTH RIDING
Vol II, 1923 p323.

YORK

See 1−3, 6−7, 19−21, 26, 30, 35, 38−40, 896, 899, 903, 906, 908, 910.

954. H.O.P.T.
1509−1558 I, p251−3
1558−1603 I, p292−5
1660−1690 I, p489−91
1715−1754 I, p364−5
1754−1790 I, p441−5
1790−1820 II, p461−4

955. KNIGHT, CHARLES BRUNTON.
A history of the city of York. 2nd ed. York: Herald, 1944.

Arranged year by year. References to parliamentary representation in index.

956. PALLISER, DAVID MICHAEL.
Tudor York. Oxford: O.U.P., 1979.

Numerous references in the index.

957. V.C.H. YORKSHIRE: CITY OF YORK
1961 p79, 139−40, 186−98, 240−5.

References to parliamentary representation scattered by period. Includes a section on boundaries and some maps.

CINQUE PORTS

See 2, 24, 26, 763, 968.

958. BURROWS, MONTAGU.
Cinque ports. 4th ed. London: Longmans, 1895.

Discusses their common parliamentary history and gives brief notes in the section on each port.

959. H.O.P.T.
1509−1558 I, p253−64
1558−1603 I, p300−7
1660−1690 I, p491−505
1715−1754 I, p365−70
1754−1790 I, p445−58
1790−1820 II, p464−80

DOVER

See **2–3, 6, 14, 16, 20–1, 23–4, 26, 30, 35, 37–40, 424, 427, 430, 958.**

960. H.O.P.T.
        1509–1558 I, p255–6
        1558–1603 I, p300–1
        1660–1690 I, p493–5
        1715–1754 I, p365
        1754–1790 I, p445–6
        1790–1820 II, p464–6

961. JONES, JOHN BAVINGTON.
Annals of Dover. Dover: Dover Express Works, 1916.

    Section VIII: Dover in Parliament, p365–406.

FAVERSHAM

See **431, 958.**

HASTINGS

See **2–3, 6, 20–1, 24, 26, 30, 37–40, 774, 958.**

962. BAINES, J. MANWARING.
Historic Hastings. Hastings: F.J. Parsons, 1955.

    Ch.7: Elections to Parliament.

963. DYMOND, T.S.
The return of barons to Parliament for the town and port of Hastings.
South-Eastern Naturalist and Antiquary, XLII, 1937 p16–23.

964. GRUENFELDER, JOHN K.
The spring parliamentary election at Hastings, 1640. *Sussex Arch. Soc. Collections,* 105, 1967 p49–55.

965. H.O.P.T.
        1509–1558 I, p256–7
        1558–1603 I, p301–2
        1660–1690 I, p495–6
        1715–1754 I, p365–6
        1754–1790 I, p446–7
        1790–1820 II, p466–8

966. V.C.H. SUSSEX
Vol IX, 1937 p12.

HYTHE

See **2–3, 6, 20–1, 24, 26, 30, 35, 37–40, 424, 427, 430, 958.**

967. H.O.P.T.
    1509–1558 I, p257–8
    1558–1603 I, p302–3
    1660–1690 I, p496–8
    1715–1754 I, p366–7
    1754–1790 I, p447–8
    1790–1820 II, p468–70

968. WILKS, GEORGE.
The barons of the Cinque Ports and the parliamentary representation of Hythe. Folkestone: J. English, 1892.

> Mostly concerns Hythe, but also contains some information about Cinque Ports in general.

NEW ROMNEY

See 2–3, 20, 24, 26, 30, 35, 37–40, 424, 427, 430, 958.

969. H.O.P.T.
    1509–1558 I, p258–9
    1558–1603 I, p303–5
    1660–1690 I, p498–9
    1715–1754 I, p367–8
    1754–1790 I, p448–52
    1790–1820 II, p470–1

970. STOKES, JOHN.
The barons of New Romney in Parliament. London: Mitchell, Hughes & Clarke, 1905. (Reprinted from *Archaeologia Cantiana*).

> In chronological order of Parliaments, with biographical notes.

RYE

See 2–3, 6, 20–1, 24, 26, 30, 35, 37–40, 774, 958.

971. H.O.P.T.
    1509–1558 I, p259–61
    1558–1603 I, p305–6
    1660–1690 I, p449–501
    1715–1754 I, p368
    1754–1790 I, p452–3
    1790–1820 II, p471–3

972. HOLLOWAY, WILLIAM.
The history and antiquities of the ancient town and port of Rye in the county of Sussex. London: John Russell Smith, 1847.

> Ch.III: The parliamentary history of Rye. Includes lists of representatives and freemen covering 1369–1832.

973. V.C.H. SUSSEX
Vol IX, 1937 p52–4.

SANDWICH

See **2−3, 6, 16, 20−1, 24, 26, 30, 35, 37−40, 424, 427, 958.**

974. GARDINER, DOROTHY.
Historic haven: the story of Sandwich. Derby: Pilgrim Press, 1954.

References to Parliament in the index. Not very helpful.

975. H.O.P.T.
1509−1558 I, p261−3
1558−1603 I, p306
1660−1690 I, p501−2
1715−1754 I, p368−9
1754−1790 I, p453−4
1790−1820 II, p473−5

SEAFORD

See **2−3, 6, 10, 20, 22, 26, 30, 35, 37, 39−40, 774−5, 958.**

976. H.O.P.T.
1660−1690 I, p502−3
1715−1754 I, p369−70
1754−1790 I, p454−7
1790−1820 II, p475−80

977. LOWER, MARK ANTHONY.
Memorials of the town, parish and Cinque Port of Seaford historical and antiquarian. London: John Russell Smith, 1855.

Parliamentary representation mentioned briefly, p17.

978. RICE, R. GARRAWAY.
Poll for the election of two barons to represent the town and port of Seaford, 25 Mar 1761. (Notes and Queries, 6). *Sussex Arch. Soc. Collections,* 44, 1901 p210−1.

Copy of an unprinted poll.

WINCHELSEA

See **2−3, 6, 14, 20, 24, 26, 30, 35, 37−40, 774, 958.**

979. COOPER, WILLIAM DURRANT.
The history of Winchelsea, one of the ancient towns added to the Cinque Ports. London: John Russell Smith, 1850.

Parliamentary history, p241−9, includes a list of representatives from 1369 to 1832.

980. H.O.P.T.
        1509–1558 I, p263–4
        1558–1603 I, p306–7
        1660–1690 I, p503–5
        1715–1754 I, p370
        1754–1790 I, p457–8
        1790–1820 II, p480

981. V.C.H. SUSSEX
        Vol IX, 1937 p68–9.

UNIVERSITIES

See **103–4, 633–4.**

982. HUMBERSTONE, THOMAS LLOYD.
University representation in Parliament. *Parliamentary Affairs*, I (1), 1947 p67–82; (2), 1948 p78–93; (4), 1948 p78–88.

983. HUMBERSTONE, THOMAS LLOYD.
University representation. London: Hutchinson & Co., 1951.

    The standard work. Contains a biographical index of university MPs.

984. REX, MILLICENT BARTON.
University representation in England 1604–1690. London: Allen & Unwin, 1954.

    Thoroughly researched. Includes a detailed index and a useful bibliography.

INDEX TO AUTHORS AND
CONSTITUENCIES

Printed for Her Majesty's Stationery Office by Commercial Colour Press, London E7. 10/86, C7, Dd.614015.